Hasenheide 13

Hasenheide 13

Lothar Uebel
Sammlung Wemhöner
jovis Verlag

Foreword

At midday on 22 March 2018, Heiner Wemhöner and
I stood for the first time in the unheated ballroom,
invisible from the street, on the grounds of Hasenheide
13. We were surrounded by mid-century furniture, neon
signs and vintage chandeliers, props for filmmaking
and other furnishings for style-conscious 'new Berliners'
searching for something special. Lovingly restored
individual pieces, treasures that had seen better days,
and all types of curiosities were piled up on metre-high
shelves: an abundance of sensory impressions that
made it almost impossible to take in the ballroom in its
entirety. And yet, Heiner Wemhöner intuitively knew
that his search had come to an end.

Our presence at Hasenheide 13 had a story behind it.
Following the first exhibition of the Wemhöner Collection
in Berlin's Osram-Höfe in spring 2014, art collector
and Managing Partner of the family-owned business
Heiner Wemhöner was inspired to find a home for
his collection of contemporary art and make it available
to the public.

Firmly convinced that Berlin was full of exceptional
properties and old factories that were simply waiting to
be awakened from their slumber, an odyssey began. It
was at times sobering, as we witnessed the major impact
that the property boom of recent years had had on the
city. Unrenovated sites that were in a suitable condition
to house and exhibit a collection of contemporary art
had truly become a rarity.

Nevertheless, our search had led us on this rainy March day to this seemingly forgotten building with its exposed brickwork that was being used temporarily as a showroom and storeroom by the furniture dealers who ran *Urban Industrial*. Their temporary use of the ballroom was intended to signal the end of a vibrant and chequered history. The building authority had already approved the demolition of the ballroom to make way for a new block of apartments. But life took a different turn.

Heiner Wemhöner did not want to let this building 'disappear', he wanted to preserve it. From then on, his focus was on a careful and painstaking restoration of the building with a view to moving in his collection and continuing the story of Hasenheide 13 as a meeting place: a story that had already begun before the building was constructed in 1899 and, in a sense, also reflected the evolution of Berlin over the last 150 years. This publication invites you to follow Lothar Uebel's research and embark on a voyage of discovery that recounts fascinating episodes in the history of an institution that has earned the right to continue bearing witness to a city that is constantly changing and evolving.

Philipp Bollmann

Introduction

In the early 1980s, I was frequently out and about between Chamissoplatz and Hasenheide in my neighbourhood of Kreuzberg, photographing historical façades or architectural details. I was particularly drawn to buildings that were at risk of demolition or whose decorative façades could fall victim to renovation. In 1984, on one of these jaunts, I came across the backyard of Hasenheide 13. On taking the photo shown below, I knew that it showed the back of the *Sector* nightclub, which I had been to and found very impressive. The architecture of the rear façade surprised me as it proved that the venue was much older than its use as a disco suggested. It was only later that I discovered that a popular Berlin entertainment venue had been located here for decades: *Kliems Festsäle.*
L.U.

The 'Cape of Good Hope'
1812—1861

Up until 1861, the site at Hasenheide 13 belonged to the village of Tempelhof, while the forested Hasenheide area that stood opposite was part of Rixdorf, modern-day Neukölln. Even then, the road from Berlin to Cottbus (today's Kottbusser Damm, extending into Hermannstraße) passed through Hermannplatz, where the Hasenheide and Urbanstraße streets now meet. The triangular tract of land between Hasenheide and Kottbusser Damm – which would subsequently become the plots for Hasenheide 1 to 20 – was known as the 'Cape of Good Hope'.

The name was clearly a nod to the cape at the southern tip of Africa, where the Dutch had established a colony that was later taken over by the British. It was a fertile area of land with many gardens and an important stopover on the way from Europe to the East Indies. A comparison was thus probably being made between this area as a point of departure from Berlin to the far south. Due to this exposed location, the first buildings were constructed at the crossroads: the *Gasthof zur Guten Hoffnung* at the corner of Urbanstraße and the *Rollkrug* inn at the southern corner of Hermannplatz. Horse-drawn carriages coming to Berlin from the south would let their wagons roll down from the *Rollberg* hills and stop off for refreshments at the public houses.

In the early 19th century, the wealthy café owner Friedrich Ludwig Pfaffenländer purchased the large meadow – presumably in 'good hope' – from Tempelhof farmers, and opened another public house on Hasenheide. Not only did he provide his guests with food and drink, he also organised special events to attract a new clientele. In 1812, the Berlin daily newspaper, the *Berlinische Nachrichten von Staats- und gelehrten Sachen* reported: 'On Wednesday, 17 June, I will host a Rose Festival at my premises. A nine-year-old girl will give a speech, and musicians on wind instruments will play Harmoniemusik every Wednesday. A summer residence will also be available to rent at said premises. Pfaffenländer in Hasenheide.' In October 1820, he announced: 'On Saturday the 14th, there will be a Wurst picnic at my premises, 8 groschen courant per person. Food will be served at 7 o'clock in the evening.' Two years later, he issued an invitation to a 'grand concert with string instruments, where someone will play the bassoon and another the basset horn'.

After *Tempelhofer Vorstadt* (to which the area north of Hasenheide belonged) was incorporated into Berlin in 1861, we find that the abstract of title in the Berlin Address Directory shows the widow Pauline Caroline Louise Pfaffenländer to be the owner of the property. The inn was already leased to a *Cafetier* (café owner) at this point.

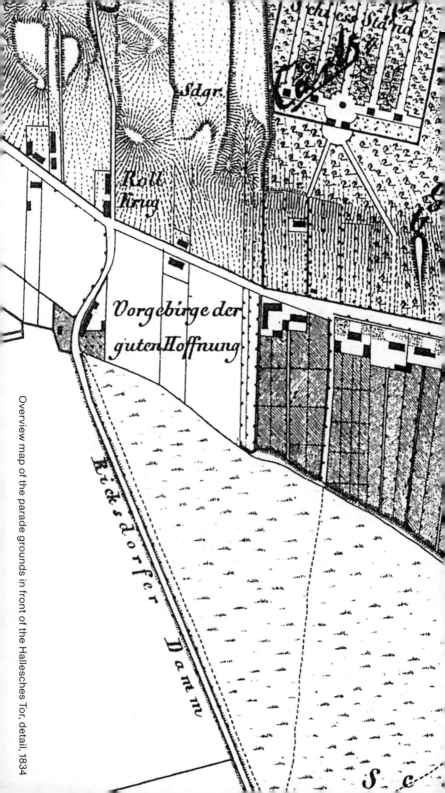

Overview map of the parade grounds in front of the Hallesches Tor, detail, 1834

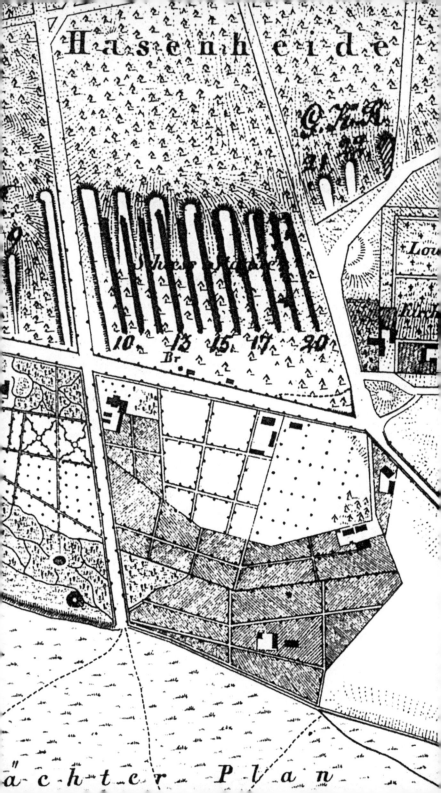

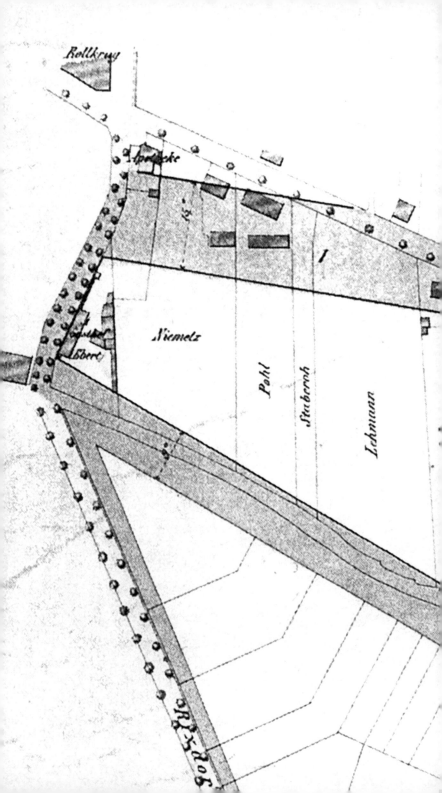

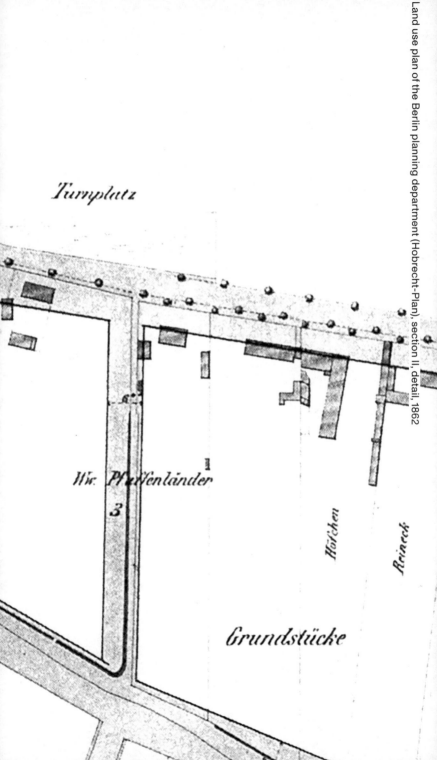

Turnplatz

Ww. Pfaffenländer

3

Höfchen

Reineck

Grundstücke

Land use plan of the Berlin planning department (Hobrecht-Plan), section II, detail, 1862

The Hasenheide entertainment district
1861—1871

The forested area got its name after a Brandenburg Elector used it as a hare enclosure for his hunting exploits. But it did not remain the sole preserve of exclusive hunting parties: in the early 19th century, Rixdorf's *Hasenheide* (hare heath) evolved into a popular country-side destination for Berlin residents. Hawkers, peep-show men, travelling entertainers, and artists soon took advantage of the thousands of people who thronged the area in their free time and began to present their wares and offer cultural experiences on the northern edge of the 'heath'. One of Berlin's first funfairs emerged from a cluster of stalls and small 'places of entertainment'.

In 1870, local historian Paul Paetel reported on the colour-ful hustle and bustle that he enthusiastically partici-pated in as a young boy with his parents. 'The pine groves extended as far as the Damm, and under the trees there was a veritable carnival atmosphere: stalls where you could play dice games, shooting galleries where you had to shoot the dumpling before it was gobbled up by the glutton. We saw the demon rising in the glass pipe, as he prophesied so beautifully; the lung-testing machine, where you blew with all your might to win a piece of hard candy on which you could really break a tooth; carousels with blacks, bays and greys and coaches so that even mother could come too. (...) There were lots of areas to dance under the trees, with the music mostly coming solely from a barrel organ or an accordion and a triangle. Only the more upmarket affairs had a few trumpet players and drums.' [1]

In 1866, we find an interesting comparison in *Garten-laube*, a popular magazine of the time: 'Even Berlin has its Hyde Park and Hyde Park amusements. In the aristo-cratic morning hours from one until three, especially on sunny winter days, elegant ladies and gentlemen stroll along the grand avenue of the Thiergarten from the Brandenburgerthor to the Hofjäger. (...) Hasenheide is the democratic counterpart to Berlin's aristocratic Hyde Park. South of Berlin lies the small spruce grove that goes by the name of Hasenheide, a "hare heath" in name only considering it has been thinned out so much that all the hares have disappeared. Now it is home to a different frolicsome crowd.' (2)

Some years later, the same magazine revealed who exactly made up this 'frolicsome crowd': those 'who seek respite after a hard week's work, minor officials, crafts-men, labourers and soldiers; with them in cosy, intim-ate alliances are young women workers, shop missies and seamstresses, servant girls and nurses.'

The throngs of people gradually attracted restaurateurs to the entertainment district, who opened coffee houses and outdoor venues. Three breweries started pro-ducing beer in Hasenheide, where they could expect strong sales of their liquid goods directly outside their front door. As the next logical step, they included large licensed premises and beer gardens on their property beside their production facilities. These offered much more than simply beer and *Bockwurst*: patrons could enjoy open-air concerts, dances, and theatre.

23

The incorporation of the area into Berlin in 1861 and
the opening of a horse-drawn tram line fuelled a
building boom: multi-storey apartment buildings now
appeared here, in the backyards of which entertainment venues of all kinds were built. Factory buildings,
on the other hand, were a rare sight.

In 1888, the author Walter Reinmar wrote: 'A street has
developed at the horse tramway from this busy life
and hustle and bustle, a curious confusion of buildings,
pleasure gardens and wooden shacks. At most, 20
to 25 years have passed since Hasenheide first endeavoured to adapt to modern life and the ever-increasing
demands of the big city. (...) As incomes have risen,
so too have people's standards. Only the clientele that
frequents the places of entertainment at Hasenheide has
remained largely unchanged. It still includes the petit
bourgeois, the workers, the military, etc., and whoever
wants to gain a thorough appreciation of people's
lives, whoever has understanding and compassion for
the less well-off, for the poorest in our society, they will
find abundant opportunities to pursue their studies
in Hasenheide. This is where they will encounter the full
river of life as it rushes up powerfully to meet them.' (3)

Kliem: A clever and resourceful restaurateur
1871—1881

Despite the throngs of Berlin residents escaping to Hasen-heide during their free time, the area was still largely uninhabited in the middle of the 19th century. As a contemporary noted: 'In 1828, 68 residents lived here in 11 (summer) houses, of which 4 were coffee gardens' (4). One of these coffee houses belonged to the restaur-ateur Pfaffenländer, whose widow was looking for a new leaseholder in 1870. She soon found one: another restaura-teur named Johann August Kliem, who acquired the '269 Ruthe parcel of land' (5) (later Hasenheide 14/15) in November 1871.

The Kliems were a married couple who came from Silesia and had already run their own inn on Berlin's Scharren-straße, which by all accounts 'went well'. While a small ballroom already existed near the inn on the property at Hasenheide, it was by no means grand enough for the new owner. He had barely acquired the land than he had submitted a planning application in the same month for a 100-metre-long hall with a bar, a 'Parisian dance salon', and toilet facilities, all of which were wooden structures on the western side of the property. He also had a garden laid out in which a stage and a hall with bowling lanes were set up.

In May 1873, the restaurateur named his entertainment venue *Kliems Festsäle*. At this time, Hasenheide was still 'j. w. d.' ('janz weit draußen' – literally quite far outside or the middle of nowhere), as they say in Berlin. But Kliem was clearly soon getting enough custom to make it worth his while to expand his premises: in 1874, he opened a new building that could accommodate 400 people on the eastern side of the property. The garden was officially permitted to admit 3,000 patrons.

From then on, Kliem had to apply each year to the Police Presidium, 'which, on behalf of the Berlin City Committee, granted me a permit to host musical performances, recitals and other theatrical shows in my garden and also in the two ballrooms on the property at Hasenheide No. 13', as it was described in the most beautiful officialese. (6)

The Kliem family lived in a 'three-girl house' (the couple had four sons and three daughters), which was located at the front of the property with a façade facing on to Hasenheide. The three girls did not have it easy, as a newspaper article around the time in 1880 remarked: 'They were three sisters. Each day, from early till late, they had to help out in the house and in the business. Mother Kliem was a great believer in tidiness and strict discipline. She was a woman cut from a particular cloth, the heart and soul of the business, who worked from the crack of dawn until late into the night. The three girls were well and truly put to work. There was no consideration given and no mercy. The three-girl house at Hasenheide was indeed a house of entertainment, *Kliems Festsäle*, but for the three girls it was no bed of roses.' (7)

'Mother Kliem: her special unit was the coffee station. At that time, there was a well-known saying in Berlin that was also often used for advertising purposes – "der alte Brauch wird nicht gebrochen, hier können Familien Kaffee kochen", which translates roughly as "the old custom is not broken, families can make coffee here". Naturally, on beautiful summer days, there were particularly large hordes of enthusiastic coffee drinkers and housewives making their own coffee. Each one was given a number, all of which were called out by Mother Kliem.

29

Rentier Kliem
Bd. 5 N⁰ 216 H u. W

Rentier Hirschel
Bd. 6 N⁰ 246 H u. W
Kliem

Restaurateur
Bielefeld
Bd. 11 N⁰ 250 H u. W

Fabrikant Schulz
Bd. 21 N⁰ 195 H u.

r Wehl u. Miteigenthümer
Bd. 1 N⁰ 10 H. u. W.

Kaufmann M
B. 22 N⁰ 311

Durch A. C. O. vom 11. Juli 1881 geneh

Fig. c. d. c. f. g. c. = 451 qm

fig. h. f. = 232 qm

hiklh = 189 qm

Figur a. b. c. a. = 3973 qm

Weichbildgrenze

Turnplatz

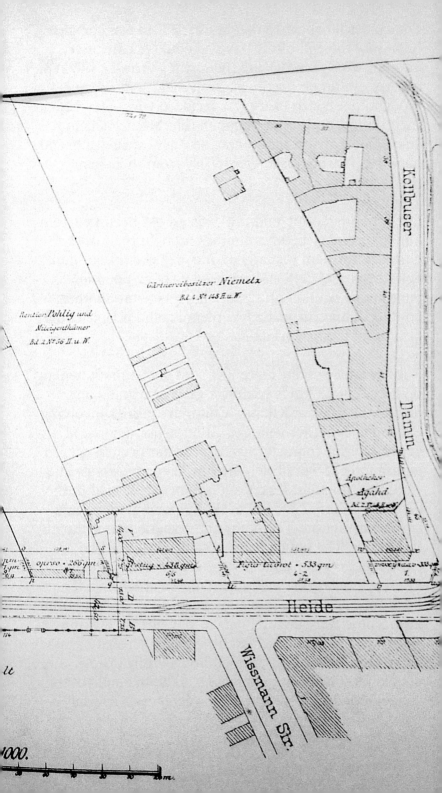

Sometimes it happened that Mother Kliem was completely hoarse by the end of the day and could hardly utter another word. But despite the jostling crowds, she kept a sharp eye on proceedings. Back then, some people thought that the crockery was included when they bought their coffee. So it might happen that Mother Kliem singlehandedly brought back the relevant suspects and conjured up the missing crockery from their baby carriages.' (7)

Such 'family coffee making' was an old Berlin custom among ordinary people: families brought their own coffee with them (usually an inexpensive mix of malt coffee and real coffee), borrowed a coffee pot and cups at one counter and got boiling water at another counter. This cost just a few pfennig, and people could also bring their own cakes.

'Sunday after Sunday there was a lot of commotion going on here. But all kinds of things were also going on during the week at Kliem's. Children's parties involving *Onkel Pelle* (author's note: a circus artist, actor, and general Berlin character) were a regular occurrence. In autumn, these were celebrated as harvest festivals and were very popular. Rakes and scythes were sold in the garden. Military concerts in the summer garden were a great attraction. The clubs and societies came during the winter. The public balls, at which soldiers had to pay 10 pfennig per dance, were very well attended. There was always something going on at Kliem's. They were enterprising people and always first with anything new. There were swing boats in the garden; a summer stage was erected on which little plays, acrobatics and chansons were performed in a joyfully chaotic mix of colours. The *Pariser Tanzplatz*, a floored and covered dance floor at the back in the garden, was a special feature and probably the first open-air dance floor. Back then, revellers spoke of going "to the Pariser", and this wooden dance floor enjoyed huge popularity.' (7)

From the beginning, *Kliems Festsäle* was also an important meeting place for Berlin's labour movement. Trade unionists and members of the Sozialdemokratische Partei (Social Democratic Party, SPD) gathered here at well-attended events. In 1878, after the *Sozialistengesetz* (Anti-Socialist Law) was passed, the military published a list of establishments that soldiers were banned from visiting, as social democrats congregated there. Kliem's was mentioned on this list, which is bound to have led to a significant loss of income for the landlord.

Meanwhile, there was a café (with or without dancing), or even a ballroom or beer garden on every plot of land on Hasenheide. Many establishments were housed on the ground floor of apartment buildings or in their backyard. In particular, at Hasenheide 108 to 114, opposite *Kliems Festsäle,* competition threatened: in 1880, the *Bergschlossbrauerei* (a Berlin brewery) had opened its large amusement park, the *Neue Welt*. In the huge ballroom and sweeping gardens, which included an 'Indian pavilion', the brewery organised spectacular events for thousands of people: local festivals with concerts, open-air theatre, tightrope walkers, and fireworks.

33

Kliem had to come up with an idea to address this situation.

For years, huge crowds had attended the social democrats' May Day celebrations for the third Berlin Reichstag constituency on 1 May in the *Neue Welt* – August Bebel spoke there in 1895, for example. Kliem's subsequently attracted a lot of visitors to its establishment, offering a 'grand open-air concert' in the garden and a 'grand ball' in its comparatively small ballrooms. However, in the long run, this was not enough to stay ahead of the competition.

Advertisements, Max Kliem's summer theatre, 1897 and 1900

A courageous step forward
1881—1899

The area around *Kliems Festsäle* changed rapidly within a few short years. After the building inspectorate decided to widen the Hasenheide street by 22 metres in 1881, the building line was also redefined. This meant that the Kliem family's old home had to be torn down (although they managed to delay this until 1906). By 1888, almost all the plots of land that had been sold off from the former large site at Hasenheide 1 to 20 had their own separate street numbers. The Kliem property now had the address Hasenheide 14/15. At this point in time, the land at Hasenheide 9 to 12 was the location of *Carl Schulz's* vast factory building. Established in 1868, the factory manufactured iron furniture. Apartment buildings that faced the street were also housed on this land. The Anti-Socialist Law was repealed in 1890 and political meetings were once again frequently held in Kliem's, which noticeably increased the occupancy of the premises.

Meanwhile, Johann August Kliem's son, Max, had taken over the running of the entertainment venue in 1889 and Johann himself died in 1897. Max Kliem clearly inherited his father's spirit when it came to business matters: within a year, he had made up his mind to purchase the neighbouring plot at Hasenheide 13 for 210,000 marks in order to complete an ambitious construction project. The seller of the 210 square Ruthe plot was a widow named Therese Hirschel, whose husband had run a plant nursery there.

Max Kliem commissioned the architect and master mason A. E. Witting to design a multi-storey apartment building and a *Saalgebäude* (a building with halls and function rooms). Witting had already made a name for himself by redesigning the *Ballhaus* (ballroom building) on Naunynstraße. The planning application was submitted in January 1899 and the construction work was completed and formally accepted by December of the same year. The end result was an impressive five-storey building with side wings, to which a narrow rear building was connected at ground level 'as an entrance structure with vestibule and buffet area'. The new 18-metre-high building 'with a bandstand' (8) towered directly behind. Iron lattice girders in the roof design ensured a flat pitched roof.

Façade design, front building Hasenheide 13, 1898

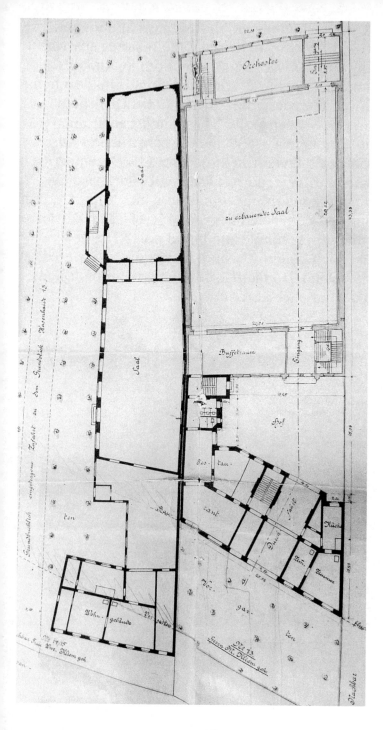

40

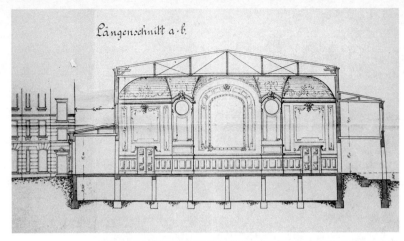

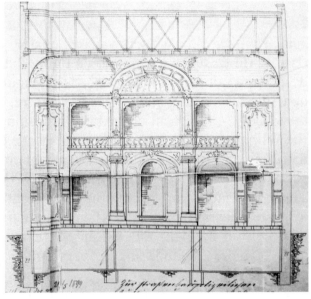

41

The architect Max Welsch was responsible for the interiors. He was also a well-known figure, having designed a number of stucco façades for multi-storey apartment buildings in Berlin's city centre. The elaborate stucco, reminiscent of the taste prevailing during the Wilhelmian era, gave the interior of the ballroom its distinctive character. As if that were not enough, a set painter was hired specially to paint two wall panels. The young Hermann Pohlmann came from Vienna and later married one of the Kliem daughters. The green area behind the ballroom extended the existing garden to the neighbouring property and could also be accessed from there.

On 10 December 1899, the proud owner of the building placed the following advertisement in *Vorwärts* (Forward), the SPD newspaper: 'I wish to announce that I will be opening my new ballroom, Hasenheide 13, with capacity for some 1,500 people, on Christmas Day. I will be making this ballroom available to esteemed clubs, societies, etc., for their festivities. At the same time, I recommend my other ballrooms for meetings and festivities

of all kinds. *Max Kliem*.' A 'Grand Winter Festival'
did indeed take place on Christmas Day. It was organised
by the social democratic electoral wing of the second
Berlin Reichstag constituency 'in Max Kliem's newly built
magnificent ballroom' with music and dancing.

Ballroom with mural, 1900

Drawing for a mural by Hermann Pohlmann, 1902

43

Picture postcard, the ballroom with final wall decoration, around 1905

Amusement, politics, and a bitter intermezzo

1900—1918

Kliem's rivalry with the *Neue Welt* on the opposite side of the street and the two large halls and beer gardens run by the breweries *Union* and *Happoldt* on Hasenheide continued. As a result, Kliem's stepped up its promotional campaigns and endeavoured to keep pace with its competitors in the entertainment it was providing. Thus, in the summer of 1900, the *Rixdorfer Zeitung* contained the following announcement: 'Sundays: Grand double concerto, theatrical and speciality performance. In all ballrooms. Grand ball.' ('Specialities' at that time were understood to be a series of variety show numbers combined with short popular plays.) During the winter season, a 'large military concert' was performed 'every Sunday in the new ballroom' by well-known regimental bands and the band, the *Norddeutsche Sänger*, appeared every Thursday.

Overview map of Berlin, detail, 1910

Business was good. At the same time, the Kliems earned additional income by renting out the apartments in the front building. According to the Berlin Address Directory, the early tenants were mainly well-off members of the middle class: a merchant, a vintner, a bank official, an auditor, a police cadet, a general agent, and even a factory owner and a manager. A bedspring cleaning shop and bicycle repair workshop shared the commercial premises on the ground floor.

When Max Kliem died at the surprisingly young age of 42 in 1906, his mother continued to run the business together with her second son. The ownership situation also changed around this time: from then on, the owners of the developed land at Hasenheide 13 to 15, with 50 per cent ownership each, were Charlotte Ernestine Eveline Kliem (the last surviving daughter of the company founder Johann August Kliem) and Eveline Christiane Helene Kliem (née Blumbecker), the widow of Max Kliem.

The old family home, the 'three-girl house', was also demolished in 1906. The two-storey house at Hasenheide 13, which also stood at the old building line and had to make way for the new apartment building, had already suffered the same fate in 1899. In their place, these properties now had front gardens that faced onto the street.

In order to be able to respond with even more flexibility to the requirements of those hiring out the various halls and to be able to accommodate an even bigger number of guests at the same event, the walls on either side of the spaces at the two adjacent properties were opened to connect the rooms. Accordingly, the following advertisement appeared in the *Rixdorfer Tageblatt* in April 1911: 'Grand ball in the three new and completely renovated ballrooms with a double orchestra and magical electrical lighting. A sight worth seeing for the dancing public. Starts at 4 o'clock. Ends at 2 o'clock. Admission fee of 20 pfennig covers admission to all 3 ballrooms.'

49

The extended area now made it a suitable premises for hosting trade fairs. For example, in May 1911, a show organised by the building cooperative *Baugenossenschaft IDEAL* presented their plans for a housing development in the Britz district of Berlin. With almost 30,000 visitors in one week and more than a thousand new members, the show proved to be a huge success, and not only for the cooperative. Thanks to the available space, *Kliems Festsäle* became a suitable multi-functional entertainment venue, and a colourful mix of events with a variety of themes took place: SPD election meetings, trade union conferences, concerts, an operetta performance of Johann Strauss's *Die Fledermaus*, and a *Jugendweihe* (coming-of-age ceremony) organised by the Free Religion parish with 'ceremonial addresses on the organ accompanied by the violin', to name but a few. There seemed to be no limit to the diversity of events on offer.

However, meetings of all kinds, whether for serious or entertainment purposes, came to an abrupt end as the First World War claimed its victims. In many towns and cities, ballroom owners were compelled by the German Supreme Army Command to make their premises available as military hospitals. *Kliems Festsäle,* now declared a reserve military hospital, was used from 1915 to care for wounded soldiers.

Interior, reserve military hospital in the ballroom, September 1914

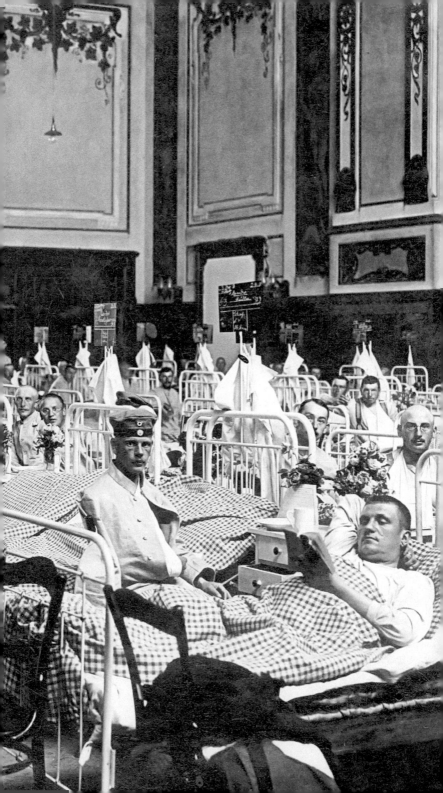

A bumpy post-war start
1919—1920

Preis 50 Pfg. (40 Pfg. und Steuer 10. Pfg.) 9

* Vergnügungs-Palast „Groß-Berlin“ * 62

vorm. Kliems Festsäle Direktion: E. Knoppe Fernspr.: Mpl. 9981

Sommer-Theater

Künstl. Leitung: Direktor Willi Walter Spanier

Programm

Direktor Willi Walter Spanier.

Vorverkaufskasse:

Wochentags von 10 – 1 und ab 3 Uhr

Sonntags ab 10 Uhr ununterbrochen

Karten stets für die nächsten 8 Tage erhältlich.

Front page of programme booklet, *Vergnügungs-Palast Groß-Berlin*, 1919

After the war, none of the remaining Kliem family members were interested in running the entertainment venue and a leaseholder was sought. The family chose experienced theatrical manager Carl Knoppe, who had been 'acquainted with the world of theatre and variety shows for decades' according to his references.

He signed a five-year agreement, paying a total annual rent of 50,000 marks for the entire establishment, including living quarters. He subsequently renamed the venue, somewhat grandiosely, the *Vergnügungs-Palast Groß-Berlin* (Pleasure Palace of Greater Berlin).

Letterhead, *Vergnügungs-Palast Groß-Berlin*, 1920

An 'artistic director' was also appointed. His name was Willi Walter Spanier, and right from the start he caused problems: the theatre police banned performances that he directed, as he did not have a permit and was on a blacklist published by the *Genossenschaft Deutscher Bühnenangehöriger* (Guild of the German Stage) on the grounds of commercial unreliability. Allegations were also made against Carl Knoppe by actors and colleagues. According to them, he was 'not irreproachable from a moral point of view'. At variety show performances involving wrestling matches, 'brawls and stabbings were the order of the day'. (6)

Apart from some unusual theatre and variety show performances, the rest of the events programme returned to normal. The trade unions gathered once again, as did the political parties. The SPD was not the only party to

Vergnügungs-Palast „Groß-Berlin"

Hasenheide 15   Kliems Festsäle   Hasenheide 15

Oberregisseure: E. Ballin, F. Herrmann

Musikal. Leitung: **Steinbock**   Konzertmeister: **W. Sieg**

Freitag, den 10. September 1920

Einmalige Aufführung
des großen sozialen Schauspiels

Die Macht der Arbeit

Ehrenabend für die Herren
Ballin, Herrmann, Widmar

Vorher:

Ein bengalischer Tiger

Schwank in 1 Akt

2 Henago's Akrobaten	**Liebesidyll** Ballet Elise Melani	**Ferry-Duett** Gesang und Tanz
4 Rudolph's Jongleure	**Bändy-Dapsang** Instrumentalist	**2 Riegelsky's** Kom. Akrobaten

Anfang: Wochentags nachm. 5 1/2 Uhr und Sonntags 5 Uhr

Vorverkauf: Täglich von 10 Uhr ab an der Theaterkasse

hold events. It was now joined by the Unabhängige Sozialdemokratische Partei Deutschlands (Independent Social Democratic Party of Germany, USPD), the Spartakusbund (Spartacus League), and shortly afterwards the Kommunistische Partei Deutschlands (Communist Party of Germany, KPD). The political debates that ensued were often acrimonious and were manifested in the world of work, such as at a meeting of striking piano workers in February 1920. Boxing matches were also held in the large hall for the first time. Mind you, these were sporting events and not yet the fistfights and brawls between social democrats and communists that were to be commonplace a few years later.

Insofar as political meetings took place, the organisers came almost exclusively from the left of the political divide. Accordingly, most of the advertising appeared as newspaper advertisements in the regional press (*Rixdorfer Tageblatt* or, from 1912, *Neuköllner Tageblatt*), in the SPD newspaper *Vorwärts* and the communist organ *Die Rote Fahne* (The Red Flag). Advertisements in the liberal *Berliner Tageblatt,* in *Berliner Morgenpost,* or even in the national conservative newspaper *Berliner Lokalanzeiger* were extremely rare. The question of the extent to which this corresponded to the political views of the restaurant proprietors must remain unanswered. The advertising was at least cleverly aimed at its target group and was clearly successful.

When the KPD convened a meeting on the subject of 'Neutrality or solidarity with Soviet Russia and the political workers' councils' at Kliem's on 31 August 1920, it appears today like a harbinger of an extraordinary phase in German theatre.

Erwin Piscator's première at Kliem's

1920—1921

On 15 October 1920 – in celebration of the upcoming third anniversary of the Russian October Revolution – the young theatre director Erwin Piscator hired the large hall at Hasenheide 13. A year earlier, at the age of 26, Piscator had moved to Berlin from Munich, where he had been an actor. In Berlin, he joined the city's Dada movement, through which he became friends with Wieland Herzfelde, his brother John Heartfield, and George Grosz.

Around 800 theatre-goers attended the première of his radical theatre project, *Proletarisches Theater, Bühne der revolutionären Arbeiter Groß-Berlins* (Proletarian Theatre, Stage of the Revolutionary Workers of Greater Berlin). The collective title for the stage show was *Gegen den weißen Schrecken – für Räte-Russland* (Against the White Terror – For the Russian Councils). The title page of the programme included artwork by George Grosz. Three one-act plays were performed: *Der Krüppel* (The Cripple) by Karl August Wittfogel, with Piscator in the lead role; *Russlands Tag* (Russia's Day) by Lajos Barta, with a set design by John Heartfield; and *Vor dem Tore* (the ambiguous title may be translated as 'Before the Fool' or 'Before the Gate') by Andor Gábor.

Not unusually for a première, there was a mishap on this particular evening, which Piscator recalled with amusement 40 years later in the presence of his friend 'Jonny' (John Heartfield): 'We had to start without your backdrop. Ten minutes into the performance, I suddenly heard you calling: Stop Erwin, stop, I'm here. The audience was uneasy, the actors stopped what they were doing. I stepped forward and said: be quiet, Jonny, we have to play on. You replied: No, I need to put up the set. And because you wouldn't let it rest, I turned to the audience and asked them whether we should continue with the performance or put up the set first. Put up the set!, called the audience. So we closed the curtains to general applause, put up the set and started the play from the beginning again to everyone's satisfaction.' [9]

Piscator brought a previously unknown theatre concept to the stage that evening, as he himself subsequently wrote: 'It was not a question of a theatre that would provide the proletariat with art, but of conscious propaganda; nor of a theatre for the proletariat, but of a

Advertisement, Proletarisches Theater, 13 October 1920

1920—1921

Proletarisches Theater

Bühne der revolutionären Arbeiter Groß-Berlins

Eröffnung am 14. Oktober 1920 mit dem Spielplan:

Gegen d. weißen Schrecken — für Sowjet-Russland

Das Prol. Theater bezweckt Einrichtungen, den Kinto..., ...halle.

Es stärkt den Willen der Massen zur ... und propagiert die proletarische Weltanschauung.

Das Prol. Theat. wird verwaltet und geleitet durch ... von seinen Mitgliedern gewählten Ausschuß in Verbindung mit ... en Organisationen.

Der Reingewinn (Überschuß) ...attierten und ...ien.

Um Mitglieder wirbt der ... Berlins f. prol. Theater.

Mitgliedsbeitrag 3 M. (Arbei... M. Eintritt f. Richtarg. 6 M.

Ausgabestellen von ... und Mitgliedskarten:

Norden
Danziger Str. 11, Alby (Cohn)
Lageler Str. 15, A. A. b. Kriegsopfer, für arbeitslose
Lninestr. 84, Metallarbeiter-Verband

Nordosten
Hochwohle 37 Doris Cohn

Zentrum
Breitestraße 6-9, Buchhandlung „Freiheit"
Klausstraße 24, Zentrale der Betriebsräte
Schiffstr. 5-6, Arbeiter-Bildungsschule
während d. Erwerbslosenamt für Arbeitslose

Osten
Lichenstraße 6, Doß
Gartenauer Str. 68, Buchhandlung Joh. Roth

Süd-Osten
...eialer 15, Buchhändler-Verband
...oralder Str. 108, „Sporthaus Roth"

Süd-Westen
Wilhelmstraße 28, IV., e-s

Nord-West: Culkenstraße 23, Rote Zeitung

Lichtenberg: Gürtelstraße 25, Buchhandlung

Neukölln: Donierstraße 24, Gläser, Cohn

Charlottenburg: Galvanistr 1, Schroeding, Cuteh

Schöneberg: ...ostel-Paulsstraße 33, Baum

Köpenick: Karola Luguß-Albertslt. 8, Jülius

Schmargendorf: Fenerbache 51, Bio-mald

proletarian theatre. We banned the word art radically from our programme. Our "plays" were appeals and were intended to have an effect on current events, to be a form of "political activity".' (10)

The director thus saw theatre as a means to an end, as an instrument of communist propaganda that could be used to initiate a revolution. Consequently, at the end of the performance, a trumpeter stepped forward, blowing a fanfare, and played the *Internationale*, which was sung not only by the choir on stage but also by the audience who joined in. The police report surprisingly noted: 'The performance was of a high artistic standard, without biased lapses or platitudes.' (6)

According to Piscator, the masses should be embraced where they live, which is why he eschewed a designated theatre building and instead gave guest performances in ballrooms in various working-class districts in Berlin. Decorative elements and costumes were reduced to a minimum, which made them easy to transport and also reduced costs, thus enabling Piscator to offer cheaper tickets to a less affluent audience. There was no hierarchy between stage hands, theatre employees, director, and actors; even the plays themselves were drafted collectively, with works by renowned authors modified on a whim. Most of the actors were amateurs. Admission prices varied from 3.50 marks for 'those organised in labour organisations' to 6 marks for the non-organised and 1 mark for unemployed people.

Although Piscator was a member of the KPD, his style of theatre was not compatible with party policy, as seen in the fulminations of one critic in *Die Rote Fahne*: 'Art is too sacred for its name to serve as a platitudinous concoction of propaganda. What the worker needs today is a strong art which sets the spirit free. Such art can be of bourgeois origin but it must be art.' (*Die Rote Fahne*, 17 October 1920)

Piscator was not to be deterred, with the result that other performances followed, at Kliem's and in other locations: Maxim Gorki's *Die Feinde* (The Enemies) was performed on 11 November 1920; Upton Sinclair's *Prince Hagen*, for which László Moholy-Nagy provided the set design, was staged on 5 December 1920; and finally, on 6 February 1921, a production of Franz Jung's *Wie lange noch, du Hure bürgerliche Gerechtigkeit?* (How much longer, bourgeois justice, you whore) was performed.

As the theatre was without a fixed abode and a regular permit to operate, official authorisations had to be obtained on a performance-related basis, something that became increasingly difficult. In April 1921, Berlin's Chief of Police finally and definitively denied Erwin Piscator a permanent permit after performances had been repeatedly banned, and Piscator had continued to proclaim that in his theatre work he subordinated the 'artistic intention to the goal of revolution'.

In the shadow of the economic crisis
crisis
1922—1926

VARIÉTÉ THEATER

Erbe

Hasenheide 13-15

Dir: Albert & Otto Erbe

Preis 20 Pf.

Front page of programme booklet, Variété Theater Erbe, 1924

If it seemed for a time that theatre and opera perform-ances would become a staple in Kliem's large hall, the tide soon turned again: the onset of the global economic crisis and the activities of political parties were com-pletely front and centre. The SPD, KPD, and their youth organisations vied with one another through lecture programmes and protest rallies. Some of these gatherings had a lasting impact, and some of them are still famous today.

On 30 July 1923, the French physicist and pacifist Paul Langevin spoke in the overcrowded hall on the theme of 'no more war'. Albert Einstein, who was also invited but was prevented from attending, sent his greetings and offered to put Langevin up at his home in Caputh.

A meeting of unemployed people organised by the KPD in October 1923 was followed by looting in the vicinity. The police report contained the following: 'After the meeting ended, a procession of 400 to 500 people made their way to Hermannplatz. The defendant, L., incited the crowd to loot, saying: Let's go and take what we need. Let's smash the windows. Like L., the defendant, G., who was also in this procession of people, also used inflammatory language and also called for the windows to be smashed. Both defendants deny the allegations but were proven guilty by two plain clothes police officers who had been monitoring the meeting.' (11) The window displays of a butcher's shop and a bakery were looted. Three perpetrators received prison sentences of several months each.

Tanz-Paradies Z E L T 2
NW 40, In den Zelten 2 (Tiergarten)
Fernsprecher: Amt Hansa 1145

E R B E
Festsäle u. Varieté-Theater
Hasenheide 13-15

Tanz-Palais Ho Bar Die
(Hofjäger-Palast)
Berlin S 59, Hasenheide 52-53

Direktion Albert & Otto Erbe

Fernsprecher: Moritzplatz 4569, 4570, 4571 ∴ Bank-Konto: Dresdner Bank, Depositen-Kasse F II, Kottbuser Damm 79
Postscheck-Konto: Berlin Nr. 85579

BERLIN S 59, den 13. Juni 24.
Hasenheide 52-53

On 28 February 1924, we read in *Vorwärts*: 'The Reichs-bund der Kriegsbeschädigten, Kriegsteilnehmer und Kriegshinterbliebenen (National Association of Disabled Soldiers, Veterans and War Dependents) had called for a protest rally to *Kliems Festsäle* to oppose the measures taken by the government under the Enabling Act (author's note: of 1923). The large hall was overcrowded long before the meeting began.'

Although the leaseholder of *Kliems Festsäle* relinquished his lease in 1924 and his successors – the brothers Albert and Otto Erbe – renamed the well-known meeting place after themselves as *Erbes Festsäle*, this did not have any implications for the programme of events. Variety shows and concerts were performed in the garden and on the open-air stage next to it; in the large hall, the events were mainly of a political hue, and politics and pleasure at times formed a close alliance.

Violent confrontations with political opponents took place for the first time at an SPD event entitled 'Down with the bread profiteers': 'Before the protest rally started, the gang of communist lads ordered to cause a disturbance gathered at Hermannplatz. They yelled: "Now we're going to take off our badges so that we can come in. (Otto) Wels is speaking at Kliem's, there's something going on there today!'" According to the newspaper report, the communist 'shock troops' had tried to disrupt the meeting 'with knives and batons and brass knuckles'. (*Vorwärts*, 1 July 1925)

In the same year, anarchists from the *Freie Arbeiter-Union* (Free Workers' Union) met in the large hall; the *Rote Hilfe* (Red Help) and *Proletarische Spielgemeinschaften Neukölln und Steglitz* (Proletarian Sports Clubs of Neukölln and Steglitz) organised an 'evening of music and entertainment'; and the *Kommunistischer Jugendverband Deutschlands* (Young Communist League of Germany, KJVD) held a Roter Rummel (Red Riot).

On 19 February 1926, around 1,000 guests listened carefully in the large hall at an event organised by the *Rotfrontkämpferbund* (Red Front Fighters' League, RFB) – a paramilitary group affiliated with the KPD – to a play that was not approved by the police. The venue owner

71

concerned said in his defence: 'We have heard that we are to be penalised by the police station because a theatre-like event was held in our large hall to mark an event organised by the *Rotfrontkämpferbund* without notifying the theatre police 14 days in advance. The RFB rented the hall from us to organise an evening of music and entertainment. Last winter, we had at least 20 or 25 of such evenings, organised on behalf of the KPD, Rote Hilfe, RFB or Internationale Arbeiterhilfe (author's note: Workers International Relief), all of which were policed by Department 1 A. We have also always notified the local police station in good time about our events and have never encountered any difficulties.

We would ask for consideration to be given to the fact that the events are without exception meetings or rallies, which, in some cases, are punctuated by recitations, speaking choruses or other performances. These types of bans, which may be seen by the organisers as one-sided, can only lead to discord and strife, whereas up to now the events have always proceeded with the utmost calm. For the reasons set out above, we would ask to be spared this punishment. We will strive in the future, provided the events (contracts) are arranged 14 days in advance, to notify Department 11 of all events and expect that said events will be policed, so that we are not once again placed in this difficult situation of being punished because a play has apparently been performed. Albert Erbe'. (6)

Bankruptcy in sight
1926—1929

The year 1926 almost heralded the death of the entertainment venue: the transport company *Berliner Nordsüd-bahn AG* endeavoured to purchase land on Hasenheide, including no. 13, for the planned expansion of the U-Bahn (underground rail) line from modern-day Südstern to Neukölln with the large interchange station at Hermann-platz. The Kliems refused to sell, but the compulsory purchase of the land was ordered by the court. Shortly afterwards, however, it was presumably deemed that less underground space was required; at any rate, the compulsory change of ownership did not take place.

Nevertheless, this did not resolve all the problems that had been threatening the venue for some time. In the autumn of 1927, the Erbe brothers closed the summer theatre at Hasenheide 14/15. Their reasons for doing this were 'firstly, the high tax burden, which is in no way commensurate with the low, keenly priced entrance tickets; secondly, the demands made by the theatre police involve huge costs that cannot be recouped over the short theatre season of just three months. Instead of the defunct summer theatre, a larger bowling alley with 20 bowling lanes and equipped with every convenience will be built, and you will see that it is our aim to make our company profitable.' (6)

When the building inspectorate opposed the bowling alley, the construction firm that had been appointed argued: 'We would like to point out that, due to the many years of construction work on the underground rail-way line, during which time traffic on Hasenheide was completely paralysed, the profitability of the existing restaurant businesses suffered so badly that Mrs Kliem is no longer in a position to sublet the premises in their current state. It is only through the construction of the planned bowling lanes, which are to be operated in conjunction with the leasing of the halls, that she can expect to get a new leaseholder.' (8)

The situation became even trickier in August 1929 when the building inspectorate demanded that a large number of defects be rectified. Failure to comply with this requirement would have incurred a penalty of 800 marks for the compulsory corrective action or resulted in a ban on the continued use of the meeting rooms. Confused, Mrs Kliem wrote to the Senior Building Officer Buck: 'I am unable to pay these costs, as the lease-holder owes me 12,564 marks in rent and taxes. The tax authorities are demanding 25,000 marks from me in balances arising for the years 1925–1928 from the tenancy of the previous leaseholder under the threat of forced administration and forced sale. My business is unprofit-able: 1. Hasenheide does not have the military per-sonnel to support a public dance business. 2. The building inspectorate closed the summer theatre as I could not pay for the required modifications and now the in-spectorate wants to ban the further use of the meeting rooms. 3. The restaurant garden has been reduced in size and the layout obstructed following the new regulations that apply in Hasenheide. How am I supposed to cover these costs and make a living? Without wanting to bore you by listing all the taxes, I have to pay: 3,014 marks for an industry tax, 16,752 marks for Hauszinssteuer (author's note: tax on rental income), 6,500 marks for rates and 16,600 marks for mortgage interest. I am selling the property and would respectfully request an extension of the deadline until after my time: the business has been in existence since 1864 and has been managed by our family with the greatest care and attention – the building inspectorate has not once had cause to enact strict regulations or measures and to this day not the slightest problem has arisen.' (8)

75

Given this situation, what occurred on 1 May 1929 was doubly tragic: this day has gone down in Berlin history as *Blutmai* (Bloody May). Police killed 33 people who took part in banned demonstrations and rallies; one of the victims was killed in *Kliems Festsäle*. Newspaper reports on events at the scene differ significantly; the report in the *Berliner Tageblatt* seems to be the most objective: 'The woodworkers held their May Day celebration in the *Neue Welt*; that was very well attended. The pipe layers, who take a more oppositional direction within the trade unions, were celebrating opposite in *Kliems Festsäle*. While the meeting of woodworkers proceeded and ended calmly, a fierce gun battle broke out in *Kliems Festsäle*. A rumour circulated that the pipe layers would form a procession after their May Day celebration had come to an end in the bar and they would hold a demonstration in the street (author's note: such activity was prohibited). Suddenly, a team of uniformed police appeared and hurried to *Kliems Festsäle* to break up the meeting. These police officers were very agitated. They must have clashed with the demonstrators. A sergeant was bleeding heavily from the face. The police officers had scarcely arrived at *Kliems Festsäle* when wild shooting began. Some 20 gunshots rang out.' (*Berliner Tageblatt*, 2 May 1929)

Under the headline 'The bloody battles of 1 May', the *Vossische Zeitung* reported on the 'most serious street disturbances since 1919' in Berlin's working-class districts. Among other things, it also led to 'clashes outside *Kliems Festsäle* on Hasenheide, where an assembly of opposition metal workers had met, most of whom were members of the Communist Party. The crowd tried to break through the police cordon, pushing officers out of the way. One of them initially fired several warning shots. This was followed by live firing, which injured three of the meeting participants.' (*Vossische Zeitung*, 2 May 1929)

The report about the pipe layers' May Day meeting in *Die Rote Fahne* makes for more dramatic reading, but is also much more detailed, suggesting that the writer was very close to the action: 'Long before 10.00 am, *Kliems Festsäle* was filled with more than 3,000 people. There was no room for several hundred others and crowds of them spilled out into the streets. The rally was scarcely over when the police, who numbered in their hundreds and were concentrated to the left and right of the premises, stormed into the hall in dense clusters, firing indiscriminately. The pipe layer Hermann Oßmann was shot in the back and collapsed in the street. Another colleague, an old pipe layer named Rödel who was sitting at the bar with his family drinking a glass of beer, was badly wounded in the arm.' (*Die Rote Fahne*, 2 May 1929)

Karstadt and the consequences
1928—1932

In June 1929, a 'cathedral of consumption' opened on Hermannplatz: the *Karstadt* architect Phillipp Schaefer had designed a colossal edifice. The monumental seven-storey building – reminiscent of US skyscrapers – with a rooftop garden and two large light towers dominated a wide expanse of the surrounding area. Four thousand employees attended to the needs of customers on a shop floor area measuring 72,000 square metres. The new department store was undoubtedly a major attraction. However, it is debatable whether it enticed a new clientele to Kliem's. If anything, the huge roof garden, where concerts and dances were hosted, was an amenity with which the pleasure palaces on Hasenheide could not compete.

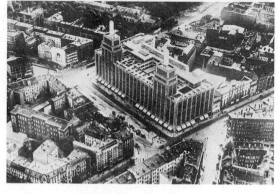

Aerial views of Hermannplatz, 1920 and 1928

Only the interchange station at Hermannplatz – which had been completed at the same time as the department store and whose underground pedestrian tunnels connected the station directly with *Karstadt* – made it easier for customers from further afield to visit the establishments on Hasenheide. Of course, the most important clients who wished to hire out the halls came, almost without exception, from the immediate vicinity.

One of these was the *Vereinigte Neuköllner Geflügelzüchter* (United Poultry Breeders of Neukölln), which in November 1929 held yet another poultry show in the large hall: 'As in previous years, the show had an extraordinary number of specimens that were well worth seeing. There were some magnificent ducks that were bred for their egg production, laying up to over 200 eggs a year. All types of chicken were on display, from the "king of chickens", the Brahma, down to the smallest, intensively bred bantam. (...) Today, there are already chickens that lay more than 300 eggs a year. It goes without saying that pigeons also featured in this show.' (*Vorwärts*, 28 November 1929)

The success of this show ultimately motivated the *Kreisverband Berliner Geflügelzüchtervereine* (District Association of Berlin Poultry Breeding Clubs) to hold its first show at Kliem's: 'Two large rooms are full, showing an orderly and well-organised assortment representing present-day poultry breeding. Fine specimens of breeding geese, Emden, Pomeranian and Toulouse geese, which have been bred extremely successfully; a splendid, huge Bronze turkey of almost half a hundredweight; many breeds of chicken, all categorised by strain, colour and breed. Hundreds of species of roosters, noble creatures, provide a concert of all timbres of rooster calls. A raffle gives visitors the chance – and hope – of bringing home

81

one of these strapping creatures if they have the winning ticket. This very handsome and informative show comes to an end this Sunday. It must honestly be a matter of pride that residents of Berlin – and especially Neukölln (which is particularly well represented) – are attending the first show of Berlin poultry breeders. It's worth it.' (*Neuköllner Tageblatt*, 23 November 1930)

One guest remembers grand end-of-term balls organised by the *Wüst* dance school, which were held at the end of dance courses in the *Saalbau Neukölln*: 'I can still see the dance teacher Wüst in front of me with his patent leather shoes and his tailcoat as he demonstrated the steps for the foxtrot. On one side were the boys, on the other side the girls. And at the end-of-term ball in *Kliems Festsäle*, each of us wore a new dress and our parents also came along.' (12)

In 1930, a theatre production, equal in quality to any of Piscator's works, caused a sensation: an ensemble of 30 male black actors, eight female black performers and three white performers presented a 'grand Negro Revue', which was supported musically by a Black jazz orchestra. It did not feature stereotypical images of Africa or discriminatory scenes showing 'savages'. Instead, this production, entitled *Sonnenaufgang im Morgenland* (Sunrise in Morningland), celebrated Black history and culture. It showed that Black people were just as 'good and bad, funny and capable' as white Europeans. (13)

'The first half of the revue, which was partly performed in an unspecified Bantu language, likely Duala, was set around 1880 and was intended to take a critical look at the effects of European colonialism on Africa from an African perspective. The second half, set in the present, was performed in French, English, and German.' (13)

Große Geflügelschau in der Hasenheide

Die "Internationale Taubenschau" in der "Neuen Welt"

In der "Neuen Welt" wurde am Freitag, im Großen Saal die "Internationale Taubenschau" von "Klub Berliner Taubenzüchter 1906 E. V." eröffnet. Unter dem Stichwort "Die führende Taubenschau des Kontingents" wurde diese Taubenschau vom Berliner Taubenzüchter-Klub ins Leben gerufen. Endlose Reihen von Käfigen füllen den großen Saal der "Neuen Welt". Ein ganzer Stab von Preisrichtern ist eifrig beschäftigt, den Taubenkäfig angebrachten Tauben die Zensuren zu geben, die jemals am Käfig angebracht sind. Die Internationalität der Taubenschau be- zieht sich auf die Tiere, da alle Arten und Rassen des In- und Auslandes, die aber

alle in Deutschland und von deutschen Züchtern gezogen sind, vertreten sind. Eine Pracht, die dem Besucher Er- staunen abringt und deren Vielgestaltigkeit an Zuchtmaterial einzig dasteht. Von der einfachsten Haustaube bis zur Pfau- und Perlücken- taube, von den herrlichsten Turteltauben bis zu den vielhundert- fältig benannten ausländischen Tauben mit all ihren charakte- ristischen Zuchtfarben- und Formen, von den zierlichsten Rassen bis zu den großen und schweren Kröpfertauben in all ihren Er- scheinungsformen und Warten, sie alle sind vertreten und machen die "Internationale Taubenschau Berlin 1906" zu einer sehens- würdigkeit allerersten Ranges. Ihr Besuch ist der letzte Tag der Ausstellung.

*

"Berolina-Schau" des Kreisverbandes Berliner Geflügelzüchtervereine

In den Räumen von Niems Festsälen, Hasenheide 13–15, er-

am Freitag nachmittag. Der erste Vorsitzende des Verbandes, Siggelkow-Neukölln, erklärte, daß aus Anlaß des zehnjährigen Bestehens der Berliner Geflügelzüchtervereine diese Ausstellung vom Verbande aus ins Leben gerufen worden sei. Der Wert ihres Bestehens sei von der Behörde, vom Staats- ministerium, den städtischen Institutionen und Landesbehörden erkannt worden und so könne er mitteilen, daß diese erste Ausstellung, die "Berolina- Schau" unter dem Protektorate des Bürgermeister Scholz stehe.

Die Ausstellung selbst ist ein Kabinettstück der Berliner Ge- flügelzüchter. Zwei große Räume sind gefüllt, die wohlgeordnet und planmäßig zusammengestellt die Vertreter unserer Geflügel- zucht aufzeigen.

Staatsexemplare von Zuchtgänsen,

Emdener, Pommersche und Toulouser Enten, die wirklichen Zucht- erfolg zeigen, eine kapitale Riesen-Bronze-Pute von bei- nahe einem halben Zentner, die vielen Rassen zusam- mengestellt nach Form, Farbe und Zuchtrasse. Sie sind der Haupt- bestand der Ausstellung. Aufgestellte Führer erklären dem Be- sucher die Rassen und Arten, geben Aufschluß über Zuchterfolg und Nutzung der einzelnen Arten. Hundert Arten von Hühnern, Bracht- tiere, führen ein Konzert auf in allen Räumen des Nachmittags. Die Ausstellung ist außerordentlich gut besetzt und gibt dem Be- sucher einen Einblick in die Arbeit des Berliner Geflügelzüchters. Wer auch einen solchen in seine Erfolge.

Eine aufgestellte Tombola gibt dem Besucher die Möglichkeit und die Hoffnung, durch ein Gewinnlos eines dieser "pfundigen" Prachttiere von den einzelnen Arten mit nach Hause nehmen zu können. Die sehr hübsche und aufschlußreiche Ausstellung nimmt am heutigen Sonntag abend ihr Ende. Es müßte geradezu Ehrensache sein, daß die Berliner und besonders Neuköllner (sie

The idea for such a Black 'race theatre' was conceived by the actor Ludwig M'bebe Mpessa – better known by his stage name Louis Brody – who was a member of the *Liga zur Verteidigung der Negerrasse* (League for the Defence of the Negro Race), which in turn was closely linked to the communist *Liga gegen den Imperialismus* (League against Imperialism). Consequently, the liberal and left-leaning press commented rather positively on the production, while a scathing article was published by the *Völkischer Beobachter* (People's Observer) the newspaper of the Nationalsozialistische Deutsche Arbeiterpartei (National Socialist German Workers' Party, the Nazi Party).

As a rule, meetings with a political message remained characteristic of *Kliems Festsäle*, as a report published in the *Neuköllner Tageblatt* about a rally to be held by the Reichsbanner (a uniformed militia that was close to the SPD) showed: 'The Neukölln Reichsbanner has launched a fortnight of promotional campaigns with the slogan *Sammlung der republikanischen Front* (Gathering of the Republican Front), starting on 30 November. In addition to the untiring efforts of officials, a Reichsbanner parade will go ahead in Neukölln this Sunday, 7 December. (...) Furthermore, a Republican ceremony will take place in Kliem's large hall on 12 December. The Berlin district chairman Johannes Stelling will speak at this rally. Moreover, the new members that are recruited during this time – the local association estimates a figure of at least 200 – will be inducted by local chairman Gutschmidt. Officials in the movement who are particularly successful will be awarded valuable book prizes. The combat sports and jiu jitsu demonstrations will bring the rally to an end, accompanied by a concert performed by the music corps of the *Reichsbanner*. Entrance to this rally is free.' (*Neuköllner Tageblatt*, 12 December 1930)

In January 1931, the KPD gathered for a large commemorative ceremony for Lenin, Liebknecht, and Luxemburg in the large hall. The agit-prop groups *Roter Blitz* (Red Lightning) and *Roter Hammer* (Red Hammer) performed, a balalaika orchestra played, and Erich Weinert read aloud a number of texts. The admission fee was 60 pfennig; half-price tickets were available for unemployed people. Later that year, in August, the hall was wholly overcrowded when the SPD called on its members to 'fight the betrayal of the people by Hitler, Hugenberg and Thälmann!'

An event organised by the Sozialistische Arbeiterpartei Deutschlands (Socialist Workers' Party of Germany, SAP) culminated in violent confrontations, an increasingly frequent occurrence: 'The meeting ended at 10.30 with a bloody brawl. For no apparent reason, the communists used chair legs, brass knuckles, and beer steins to beat the mostly young Seydewitz supporters, who could barely defend themselves against the superior strength of the communists. The police finally had to break up the meeting and clear the hall using force.' (*Vorwärts*, 23 October 1931)

Meanwhile, the leaseholder had changed once again. Alfred Trzezakawski, the successor to the Erbe brothers, was clearly less vain and in 1931 decided to change the name back to *Kliems Festsäle*. The mix of events remained unchanged. Bookings were up, and the *Karstadt* roof garden had lured very few patrons away. A look at the programme for 1932, for example, provides an almost seamless insight into the mix of events that were typical of the Kliem establishment throughout its long history.

In the year before radical changes took hold, there was proof that the following events took place:

16 January 1932
Charity event that included the performance of a revue by the *Arbeitersportverein Fichte* (Fichte Workers' Sports Club)

19 January 1932
Rally for the *Eiserne Front* (Iron Front)

February 1932
Roter Karneval (Red Carnival), a politically satirical event organised by the SAP's *Sozialistischer Jugendverband* (Socialist Youth League, SJV)

'The hall was so overcrowded that the main entrance had to be locked and the dance floor, which had foolishly been cleared, was blocked again in next to no time. More than 1,700 participants – hundreds had to be turned away – forged ahead, shoulder to shoulder, blocking the narrow passageways between the rows of tables, lining up against the walls and laying siege to the entrances. In terms of presentation, a great deal had been achieved in the hall at very little cost. Razor-sharp caricatures of contemporary characters hung along the walls, their faces contorted into ugly grimaces. The artistic high-point was reached with the workers' songs of Ernst Busch. The three songs – unfortunately only three! – were met with rousing applause that lasted several minutes in the tightly packed hall. Other than that, following the end of the political programme, the audience managed to make space for a dance floor despite the improbably cramped conditions.' (SAP official newspaper, 1 March 1932)

7 March 1932
Event organised by the *Verband proletarischer Freidenker*
(Association of Proletarian Freethinkers): 'The cultural
decline of the working population and the presidential
election'

20 March 1932
Charity event that included the performance of a revue
by the *Arbeitersportverein Fichte* 'with a concert, dance
and other merrymaking', at which the net proceeds
benefitted workers who had been laid off at the
Ullstein publishing house

12 April 1932
Event organised by the SAP: 'Proles, intervene! Workers'
Front against fascism!'

23 April 1932
'Cabaret of the worker-actors'

18 May 1932
KPD meeting at which an SAP member distributed
leaflets at the Hasenheide entrance with the title 'KPD
workers, how should the united front be created?'
Not only was he reviled and verbally abused by the communists as a blackguard and scoundrel, he was also
arrested by the police as he had distributed a flyer that
had not been approved by the police authorities. (Such
approvals had been required due to an emergency decree
that had been enacted as a result of the increasingly
aggressive political antagonism between the parties.)

2 June 1932
Meeting of plasterers organised by the *Deutscher
Baugewerksbund* (German Union of Building Trades)
in the large hall

91

Socialist Labour Party (SAP) poster on an advertising pillar, April 1932

8 July 1932
Meeting of the *Rote Einheitsfront* (Red United Front) organised by the KPD

21 July 1932
Works councils plenary meeting of the *Groß-Berliner Betriebsräteausschuss* (Greater Berlin Works Councils Committee) at the invitation of the KPD to prepare for a 'mass strike'

28 July 1932
SAP event: 'SPD – KPD – SAP must march together!'

September 1932
Tenants' conference with 1,000 delegates to discuss the continuation of the tenants' strike, which had begun in July and by September had attracted more than 30,000 tenants

13 October 1932
KPD event

16 October 1932
'Mass rally' organised by the *Internationaler Bund der Opfer des Krieges und der Arbeit* (International League of Victims of War and Work)

21 October 1932
'Meeting of public workers' organised by the *Deutschnationaler Arbeiterausschuss Neukölln* (German National Workers' Committee of Neukölln)

3 November 1932
Unemployment rally in the large hall

SPD · KPD · SAP
müssen gemeinsam marschieren!

Oeffentliche Versammlung

am Donnerstag, 28. Juli 1932, 20 Uhr
Kliems Festsäle, Hasenheide

Referent: **Sternberg**

Unkostenbeitrag 20 Pf.   Erwerbslose 10 Pf.

Sozialistische Arbeiter-Partei, Ortsgruppe Neukölln u. Kreuzberg

Rentenempfänger!

**Kriegsbeschädigte
Kriegshinterbliebene
Kriegereltern und -Waisen
Unfall- und Invalidenrentner
Tumultbeschädigte
Wohlfahrtsempfänger
Blinde und Taubstumme
Erwerbslose, Betriebsarbeiter**

Heraus zur
Massenkundgebung

Freitag, den 16. Oktober, 19 Uhr, Kliems Festsäle
Hasenheide

Es werden sprechen:

Hugo Gräf, M. d. R., Bundesvorsitzender
Leiter der intern. Invaliden-Delegation nach der U.d.S.S.R.

Hans Tilke, Stadtverordneter
Leiter des Gaues Berlin-Brandenburg

über die Themen:
Die Versorgung der Kriegs- und Arbeitsinvaliden
und deren Hinterbliebenen in Deutschland und in
Sowjetrußland
Abbau der Fürsorge u. Wohlfahrt in den Gemeinden

Freie Aussprache

Die Gauleitung des Zentralverbandes der Arbeitsinvaliden, Gau Berlin, und
die Gauleitung des Reichsbundes der Kriegsbeschädigten und Kriegshinterbliebenen, Gau Berlin, sind zu dieser Veranstaltung schriftlich eingeladen

Internationaler Bund der Opfer des Krieges und der Arbeit E.V.
(Deutsche Sektion) Gau Berlin-Brandenburg, Neue Friedrichstraße 38-40
Ortsgruppe Kreuzberg Abteilung I, Reichenberger Straße 111, Abteilung II, Gneisenaustraße 35
Ortsgruppe Neukölln, Donau- Ecke Erkstraße

Arbeiter! Kommt und hört!

Freitag, 13. November, abends 8 Uhr, Kliems
Festfäle (kleiner Saal), Berlin, Hasenheide 13-15

Große öffentliche

Arbeiter=Versammlung

Es sprechen: Arbeiter Stadtrat **Paul Schönstedt**, Potsdam, über:

Der deutsche Arbeiter in den Kämpfen dieser Zeit

Bundesvorsitzender **Wilhelm Schmidt**, M. d. R., über:

Wir fordern Freiheit, Arbeit, Recht!

Freie Aussprache

Eintritt 20 Pf.
Erwerbslose 10 Pf.

Die Neuköllner Arbeiterschaft, die verantwortungsbewußt mitarbeiten will
an der Gestaltung ihrer Zukunft, wird um zahlreiches Erscheinen gebeten

Verantwortlich für Inhalt und Druck:
Reichseingeldg. Wilh. Schmidt, Neukölln, Parselstr. 45

Arbeiterausschuß Neukölln der DNVP.

Drel-Druck, Berlin SW 16, Ordasts. 10/11

Arbeiterschicksal
im neuen Reich

Freitag, den 21. Oktober 1932, abends 8 Uhr,
findet in Kliem's Festfälen, Neukölln, Hasenheide 13-15

eine öffentliche

Arbeiterversammlung

statt. In derselben werden sprechen

Reichsminister a. D. **Dr. Koch=Elberfeld** und
Bundesvorsitzender **Fritz Heß**, Berlin=Lichterfelde

Wir laden hierdurch die gesamte Arbeiterschaft von Neukölln zu dieser bedeutsamen
Veranstaltung ein, um zu hören, was die vorgenannten beiden nationalen Arbeiter-
führer über das Thema „Arbeiterschicksal im neuen Reich" zu sagen haben

Zur Deckung der Unkosten
werden 20 Pf. Eintritt erhoben
Erwerbslose zahlen 10 Pf.

Deutschnationaler Arbeiterausschuß Neukölln
Wilh. Schmidt, Vorsitzender

8 November 1932
Amateur film screening by the *Reichs-Radium-Gesell-schaft* (Reich Radium Society)

18–20 November 1932
Pigeon show organised by the *Reichsverband Deutscher Taubenzüchter* (Reich Association of German Pigeon Breeders)

9 December 1932
Amateur play, *Glaube und Heimat* (Faith and Homeland), performed by the Galilee parish in Neukölln, at which the admission fees were intended to pay for Christmas presents for poor people

10–15 December 1932
Event to prepare a Christmas market on Ebert-Platz with stands, music and entertainment, and bands with unemployed artists

Apparent normality despite dictatorship
1933—1941

ETABLISSEMENT
KLIEM'S FESTSÄLE

Spezial-Ausschank Engelhardt-Brauerei

Festsäle ◆ Konzertgarten ◆ Restaurant ◆ Vereinszimmer

Fernsprecher:
F6, Baerwald 6565

Berlin S. 59, den *14. Mai 19 3...*
Hasenheide 13/15

An
die städt. Bauzolizei
zu
Berlin
Yorkstr. 11.

STADT BERLIN
BEZIRKSAMT KREUZB
Eing: 15. MAI 30
STELLE:

ETABLISSEMENT
KLIEM'S FESTSÄLE
Inh.: Alfred Trzezakowski

Spezial - Ausschank Engelhard - Brauerei

Festsäle ☐ Konzertgarten ☐ Restaurant ☐ Vereinszimmer

Fernsprecher :
Amt F 6 Baerwald 6565

STADT BERLIN
BEZIRKSAMT KREUZBERG
Eing. 7 AUG 33 V.
STELLE:

BERLIN S. 59, den 5. August 1933.
Hasenheide 13/15

An

die Städt. Baupolizei Kreuzberg,

Berlin SW.
= = = = = = = = = =
Yorckstr. 1o-11.

Etablissement Kliem's Festsäle Berlin SW 29
Inh. Alfred Trzezakowski

Spezial - Ausschank Engelhard - Brauerei

Festsäle ◯ Konzertgarten ◯ Restaurant ◯ Vereinszimmer

Fernsprecher 66 65 65

Berlin SW 29, den 25. Mai 1937.
Hasenheide 13 - 15

Bezirksbürgermeister
Verwalt. Bezirk Kreuzberg
Eing. 25. MAI 1937 N
Stelle: .... Unt.

Baupolizei Bezirksamt Kreuzberg,

Berlin SW.
= = = = = = = = = =
Yorckstr. 1o-11.

The Nazis' seizure of power on 30 January 1933 and the persecution of political opponents was initially reflected directly in the topics covered at the meetings. On 3 February 1933, the KPD called for a rally in the large hall against the 'Hitler-Papen dictatorship'. Two days later, the 'Greater Berlin Tenants' Conference' met at Kliem's where a 'further deterioration in the situation under the now ruling national socialist regime was forecast. Apart from that, however, the same old rallying cries and demands were repeated, and calls for a tenants' strike continued to be made. The Berlin tenants' movement that was active during the global economic crisis was therefore a victim of the very same helplessness that had gripped the German workers' movement as a whole in the face of its imminent destruction by the national socialists – and it had similarly failed.' (14)

On 10 February 1933, a large youth rally called by the *Kommunistischer Jugendverband* (Communist Youth League, KJV), *Sozialistische Arbeiter-Jugend* (Socialist Workers' Youth, SAJ), and the *Reichsbanner* was attended by over 2,000 people. *Die Rote Fahne* reported in detail on the event. Two days later, the KPD organ was banned for 14 days and was subsequently only published one last time on 26 February 1933 before Karl Liebknecht House, the KPD's headquarters, was occupied and closed down by the Nazi *Sturmabteilung*, the SA. One of the SPD's last approved campaign events in Berlin was a 'rally for women voters' on 22 February. This took place in both overcrowded halls, accompanied by a concert provided by a *Reichsbanner* band. A works council plenary meeting did take place on 27 February 1933, entitled 'How do we make the united front a reality – ADGB, SPD, KPD and RGO' are invited', (15) but this was one of the last major events undertaken by

101

Theater-Verein   „Freie Kunst 09"

PROGRAMM

Sonntag, den 5. November 1933

in Kliems Festsäle, Hasenheide 13 (Gartensaal)

Konzert   Theater   Tanz

Eröffnung 3 Uhr   Anfang des Konzerts 4 Uhr

Beginn der Vorstellung 5½ Uhr

Eintritt inkl. Steuer und Tanz: 0,75 Mk.   Erwerbslose: 0,50 Mk.

I. TEIL:

Konzert, ausgeführt von dem Orchester-Verein
„Allegro 1889", unter Leitung seines Dirigenten E. Dochow
zirka 45 Mitwirkende

1. Victoria, Marsch . . . . von Blon
2. Ouvertüre „Die Felsenmühle" . . . . von Reissiger
3. Czardas aus der Oper „Der Geist des Wojwoden . . . von Großmann
4. Präludium, Chor und Tanz aus Operette „Das Pensionat" . von Suppe
5. Herbstweisen, Walzer . . . . von Waldteufel

II. TEIL: Theater. Zur Aufführung gelangt:

„Die Rosen-Mühle"

Singspiel in drei Akten. Text und Musik von E. Brüning

PERSONEN:

Christian Bach, Besitzer der Rosen-Mühle . . . Kurt Thürnagel
Gertrud, seine Tochter . . . . Martha Franz
Rose, Wirtschafterin bei Bach . . . . Hildegard Mieth
Walter Frank, Müllergeselle . . . . Walter Gregor
Hans, Müllerlehrling . . . . Margarete Elwers
Käte ⎫ Gertruds Freundinnen . . . . Frida Gregor
Dora ⎭ . . . . Gerda Brockhoff
Florian ⎫ Forstgehilfe . . . . Bernhard Graebe
Dietrich ⎭ . . . . Bruno Behl
Ein Postillon . . . . Erich Herzke
Zwei Bauernmädchen ⎰ . . . . Elli Dalkowski
⎱ . . . . Fridel Berger
Zwei Müllergesellen ⎰ . . . . Kurt Brückner
⎱ . . . . Marga Behl
Ein Bauernknabe . . . . Ingeborg Mieth
Bauern und Bäuerinnen . . . . Mitglieder des Vereins

Ort der Handlung: Ein märkisches Landstädtchen.   Zeit: im Jahre 1900.

Regie und Tänze: Hildegard Mieth

Bühnenbau: Bernh. Graebe   Inspizient: Kurt Heinze

Kostüme liefert E. Mieth, Nkln., Bergstr. 147   Friseur: Schaumann, Hermannpl. 6

102

the free trade unions. Time had run out for the creation of the anti-fascist alliance that was urgently needed.

After the SPD, KPD, and unions were banned and political opponents were violently swept away, events that were supportive of the regime replaced the prevailing political agenda at Kliem's. Otherwise, everything seemed to continue as before; a terrifying normality set in. In addition to a rabbit show organised by the *Reichsverband Deutscher Rexkaninchenzüchter* (Reich Association of Rex Rabbit Breeders), an exhibition of electromedical equipment with slideshows, a settlers exhibition organised by the publisher *Siedlung und Landhaus* (Settlement and Country House), and an evening of theatre staged by the *Freie Kunst 09* (Free Art 09) theatre club, a 'social evening' arranged by the local Wildenbruchplatz group of *Nationalsozialistische Kriegsopferversorgung* (National Socialist War Victims Care, NSKOV) and an event organised by the *NS-Volkswohlfahrt* (National Socialist People's Welfare, NSV) also took place.

Other than that, boxing matches were frequently held by the *Box-Sport-Club Neukölln* (Neukölln Boxing Club) with more than 600 spectators in the large hall, and films were screened by the *Deutsche Arbeitsfront* (German Labour Front, DAF) and the district film office controlled by the Nazi Party. In 1935, Otto Kermbach's orchestra, famous for its *Sportpalastwalzer* (Sportpalast waltzes), even played a concert to a hall that was filled to overflowing. In 1938, choir members came together for a choral competition organised by the *Sängerkreis Berlin* (Berlin Choral Society).

Just three months before the outbreak of the Second World War, one could be forgiven for thinking that time had rushed by, leaving *Kliems Festsäle* unscathed: in June 1939, the *Musikverein Echo Neukölln 1894* (Echo Neukölln 1894 Music Society) issued an invitation to a garden concert with a variety show and dancing on a poster that dated back to shortly after 1900; a large quantity of the posters had clearly been preprinted at that time. The invitation still used an art nouveau typography, but a new date had been added.

Programme note, Echo Neukölln 1894 Music Society, 1939

The early war period had a distinctly negative impact on the hiring of the halls. Fewer and fewer people were in a mood to celebrate. In 1941, the then-owner of the building, Charlotte Friese (née Kliem), was seeking a buyer. *Engelhardt Brauerei AG* proved to be a suitable candidate. The brewery was prepared to pay 485,000 reichsmarks. However, any likely plans to continue using the building in the same way it had been used before clearly came to naught: the large hall was used as a warehouse to store steel until the end of the war.

0,30 ...utsche Arbeitsfront

»Kraft durch Freude« / Amt Feierabend und
Amt Deutsches Volksbildungswerk

...RITTS-KARTE

...eitungsschau des Kreises X

»Nach der Arbeit«

am 20. und 21. Mai 1939 / »Kliems Festsäle«
Berlin SW 29, Hasenheide Nr. 13–15

003679 ✳

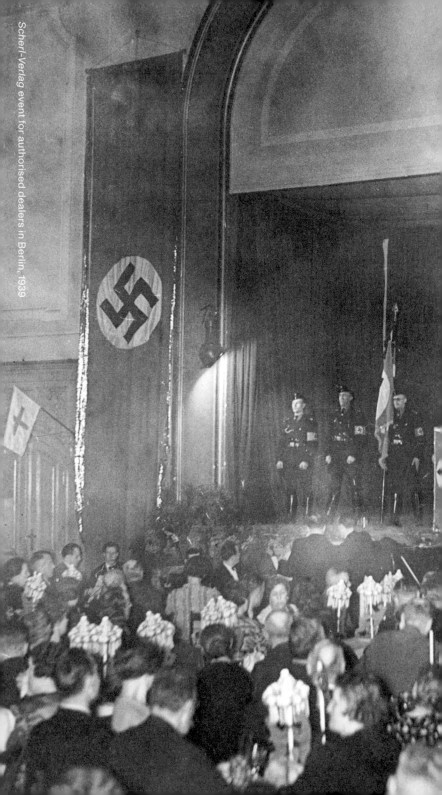

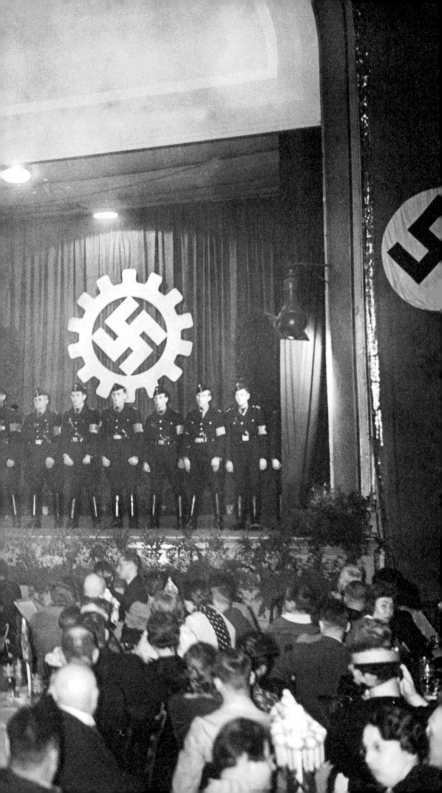

Hitler's birthday cake being handed out, 1939

New beginning as a cinema complex
1946—1951

Quick

AM HERMANNPLATZ, HASENHEIDE 13

Programm

mit
Film-Vorschau

Die Aussenausstattung dieses Theaters
führt aus

ATELIER

Dekoration FREIGANG Malerei

BERLIN W9 POTSDAMERSTR. 10 NÄHE POTSDAMER PL.
NEUKÖLLN, MAINZER STR. 8 NÄHE HERMANNPLATZ

Although the buildings at Hasenheide 14/15 had been damaged by bombing, the small halls were soon refurbished and used for various types of events. However, it seemed to be commercially futile to use the large hall on the neighbouring property at Hasenheide 13, which had remained largely undamaged, as a ballroom. As a result, the *Engelhardt* brewery decided to have it converted into a cinema.

Designed by architect Karl Waske, the *Quick* cinema opened in 1946 with more than 800 seats. Tickets for the screenings sold like hot cakes, and the number of seats in the cinema auditorium was increased to 940 just one year later.

However, the proximity to the apartments in the front building proved to be problematic. In August 1948, a tenant complained about the 'deafening noise' coming from a generator set up in the courtyard that produced electricity for the projection room. 'It would have been possible to set up the machine at a location where the tenants of two buildings would not have their night's sleep disturbed. For me personally, it is impossible to use my study (on the first floor, facing the courtyard) for any productive work, as the noise from this machine can be described as nothing less than nerve-racking.' [8] However, given the frequent power outages during the Berlin Blockade, the emergency generator was deemed 'vital' for the cinema operator, which is why its continued use was authorised by the building inspectorate.

For many Berlin residents, going to see a film was the
most popular diversion after the war. As a result, the few
cinemas in the city were bursting at the seams. The
Quick cinema – in what was formerly Kliem's large ballroom – still offered considerable potential for expansion.
This opportunity was finally seized and the renowned architect Fritz Wilms, who specialised in cinemas, was
commissioned to convert the building into a large cinema
with more than 1,000 seats. In October 1949, the *Primus
Palast* opened. A cinema of the same name had previously
stood at Urbanstraße 72 to 76. (The cinema on Urbanstraße had opened in 1928 beside the *Karstadt* department
store and had been destroyed in the Second World War.)

In 1951, the stucco on the façade of the apartment building
at Hasenheide 13 was chipped off and replaced with
a smooth plaster finish – an act which, from a modern
perspective, is both incomprehensible and regrettable.
However, it must be remembered that the country was
still in post-war mode. In many cases, homeowners
did not have the money to restore damaged façades. At
any rate, the restoration of lavishly decorated stucco
features was not deemed possible at that time, which is
why the Senate launched a programme that subsidised
the removal of the stucco and its replacement with
smooth plaster. This meant that at least the apartments
could be kept dry and the heat could be retained more
effectively, as fuel was in short supply.

It is unclear, however, whether these reasons pertained in the case of the façade at Hasenheide 13. The *Engelhardt* brewery may have had the means to finance a more meticulous restoration. However, the prevailing taste also played a significant role: the lavishly stuccoed façades of the Wilhelmian era were seen as 'old-fashioned', and many people had a preference for clean, Bauhaus-inspired lines, a trend that had already begun to take hold in the 1920s.

Another reason for the smooth plaster in this case was the specific requirement for a modern cinema façade. The impressive entrance to the multiplex cinema had a portico with the name written on it in the form of a neon sign; its colour was also intended to attract attention. The *Primus Palast* 'stands out thanks to its bright paintwork, creating a striking outline around the entrance area inside the façade of the apartment building. The two glazed front doors, flanked on either side by display cases, are crowned by an almost monumental-looking neon logo. To the right, a large advertising panel attracts visitors.' [16]

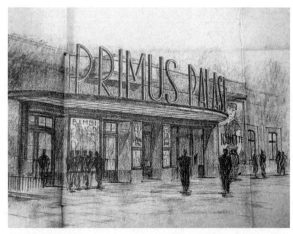

Construction drawing for *Primus Palast*, 1951

115

While the auditorium was imposing in terms of size,
it had a very unpretentious design: 'The auditorium
features a variety of seating options, with both folding
wooden chairs and upholstered armchairs, reflecting
the different price ranges. At the back of the auditorium,
a balustrade separates the slightly inclined box seating
area from the rest of the space. The light fittings are
draped in panels of fabric, giving relief to the mono-
chrome walls, whose lower sections are covered in wood
panelling.' (16)

The cinema programme included all the popular films
of the time, with Hollywood being the main supplier.
As *Neues Deutschland* – the main organ of the Sozialistische Einheitspartei Deutschlands (Socialist Unity Party
of Germany, SED) – indignantly reported in 1952, 'Blood-
thirsty American gangster films' were frequently shown.

Prominent political speakers in the auditorium
auditorium
1948—1975

Willy Brandt

spricht am 7. Febr. 1963 um 19.30 Uhr in Kliems Festsälen Hasenheide

Ab 18.00 Uhr spielt die Kapelle Bruno Wedekind

A married couple, Fritz and Anneliese Otto, had leased the entire establishment at Hasenheide 13 to 15 in April 1948. Fritz Otto was a member of the SPD and, later, Vice Guild Master of the Berlin Hospitality Guild. 'As a comrade, after the war, (author's note: he) adopted all the old Hasenheide traditions. His ballrooms were once again a place for party meetings. Louise Schroeder (a prominent SPD politician and governing mayor of West Berlin in 1947/48) planted a lilac tree in front of the venue as a sign of a lightsome new beginning. All eminent social democrats congregated at Kliem's.' (*Der Tagesspiegel*, 18 February 2001)

Otto Suhr, Ernst Reuter, and Willy Brandt were regular guests at SPD conferences. High-profile CDU politicians, such as Jakob Kaiser and Kurt Georg Kiesinger, could also be seen at the rostrum. At a trade union meeting held on 26 May 1946, everyone was agreed that the 'trade unions would not (author's note: be allowed to) be the auxiliary forces for the victory of communism'. This event was so overcrowded that Allied officers had to prevent additional visitors from entering.

Meanwhile, a variety of other events took place: boxing and wrestling matches organised by private promoters, Whitsun concerts, May Day celebrations, club anniversary celebrations, and a carnival ball, whose theme was 'There's music in Rixdorf'. People also met for gatherings that today would seem unimaginable, such as the 'Parliamentary Beer Evening' organised by the members of the Kreuzberg district council in November 1954.

Louise Schröeder

spricht zur Kreuz<u>berger</u>
<u>Bevölkerung</u>

Freie Aussprache

am Dienstag, dem 7. November 1950
um 19.30 Uhr in »Kliems Festsälen«
Hasenheide 13, in einer

öffentlichen Versammlung

Sozialdemokratische Partei Deutschlands · Kreis 6, Kreuzberg

Öffentliche
Wahlversammlung
CDU
der

Es sprechen:

Ernst **Lemmer**

Hermann **Drewitz**

FREIE AUSSPRACHE

Freitag, 3. Nov. 20 Uhr

Kliems Festsäle, Hasenheide 13

Christlich-Demokratische Union Deutschlands
Landesverband Berlin

Gerlachdruck Berlin SW 61

125

An employee at the Neukölln-based damper factory *Hasse & Wrede* commented on a Christmas party that was held for the company's workers: 'It was 1956, all the staff and their families were there. There were a few performances, including a carnival group with their carnival princess, who danced and hopped around in various costumes. Afterwards, there was dancing for everyone. Unfortunately, the company subsequently gave up on these parties as there had been a punch-up at that one.' (17)

The final changes in leaseholder in 1963 and 1970, could not turn things around: business was going from bad to worse, and in 1967, the *Engelhardt* brewery found a leaseholder for the property at Hasenheide 13, who, as we will see, had plans for something completely different. At Hasenheide 14/15, the politics and pleasure business drifted along for another few years. The 100th anniversary of *Kliems Festsäle* was even celebrated by more than 500 guests on 10 May 1973. The end finally came in 1986, and the small halls made way for a hotel two years later.

Cheetah — a futuristic temple of dance

1968—1983

Starting in the early 1960s, a new type of youth culture from London had also established itself in West Berlin: people danced to records playing beat music and called these entertainment venues discothèques (discos for short). The *Dachluke* had been going on Mehringdamm since 1961 and the *Big Eden* had just opened on the Kurfürstendamm when the new leaseholder took over the large hall at Hasenheide 13. Werner Lenke had something planned that Germany had never seen before: the architect Lothar Busch provided him with drawings for a spectacular disco, which he initially called by the old-fashioned name 'Tanzgaststätte Hasenheide' (Hasenheide dance hall). Soon, however, a suitable name was found, and in 1968 work began to convert the *Primus Palast* cinema into the *Cheetah* disco.

The two main construction companies involved, the consulting engineers *Rosenthal & Bartels* and *Peiner Stahlbau GmbH*, together with 50 other companies, faced a daunting challenge that they rose to with great success: computers were even used to deal with the complexity of the work. Stainless steel struts – weighing 200 tons and mounted at an angle with 18 round platforms on top – projected into the hall, utterly changing the look of the room. The conversion cost several million deutschmarks.

The description in the colourful prospectus did not exaggerate: 'The speed of the cheetah (…) makes it unique among its fellow animals. The *Cheetah* is also unique in its construction and architecture. It is Europe's most modern dance and entertainment centre. Berlin has certainly gained a genuine attraction. Two stainless steel tunnels provide access to the interior, which measures 850 square metres and boasts ceilings 13 metres high (there is capacity for about 2,000 people). The almost utopian DJ's booth can be extended to a height of 9 metres. Bands alternate with DJs playing the latest hits. All the cables controlling the lighting effects converge here.

Interior views of *Cheetah* featuring live band,1970

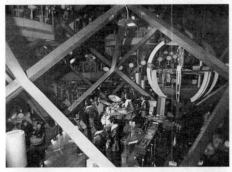

The coloured lights on the dance floors and the parabolic mirrors on the walls are synchronised with the music. The *Cheetah* hosts only the top international bands and show orchestras. Artists play for a month, with intermittent performances by current stars or up-and-coming names in show business. The circular podium at the centre of the room is 6 metres in diameter and is big enough to accommodate twelve artists. A total of six dance floors are distributed across the space and on the upper platforms. On entering the space, you are greeted by a whole panoply of shapes and colours.

133

134

Due to the venue's vast size and ingenious design, with platforms projecting into the open space, it is impossible to take it all in straight away. The platforms – circular seating and dance areas, tiered over several levels – are supported by a stainless steel frame. They are connected to one another by steps and offer a completely new sense of space. The seating and the light fittings are custom-made and create an aura of extravagance. Guests have a choice of five televisions and can relax in upholstered recliners as they watch their preferred programme.'

Advertisement, Cheetah, 1969

The launch featured live music from *Pink Floyd* – 'really, believe it or not!' wrote one contemporary witness later – and the then-German Schlager star *Ricky Shayne*, who performed his hit song *Ich sprenge alle Ketten* (I bust all the chains). The response from the media was overwhelming and young people came in their droves. 'With a metallic tunnel entrance, a futuristic interior, seven dance floors on individual levels and space for 2,000 people, the *Cheetah* has caused a furore beyond Berlin's city limits. People have stood in queues. (...) An architect has been allowed to let his imagination run free and the building inspectorate has even accepted it.' (18)

Despite the unique furnishings and the exclusive music offering, the entrance charge and drinks prices were not exorbitant: admission on Mondays and Tuesdays cost just 1 mark, while Wednesdays, Thursdays and Sundays it was 2 marks, Fridays 3 marks and Saturdays 5 marks. An Engelhardt Pilsner cost 2.50, a Coca Cola was 2.20, and a bottle of Söhnlein Brillant sparkling wine could be had for 25 marks. In the early days, there was a strict dress code: jeans were frowned upon and men were not admitted without a tie.

At weekends, the live bands came on early in the evening and were followed by a disc jockey who then took over. Many of the bands that played back then are long forgotten, but some of them were top acts. For example, in 1969, the Berlin band *Birth Control* and the British outfit *Marmalade*, whose single *Ob-La-Di, Ob-La-Da* had been number one in the charts that year, graced the stage at the *Cheetah*.

Once again, the proximity to the residents in the nearby front building proved to be problematic: in February 1969, tenants complained about excessive noise and the leaseholder was forced to install soundproofing materials in the area facing the courtyard – on doors, in the air conditioning system, and in the lift. He also asserted that 'in contrast to the beat bands that were engaged at the start, bands who can be expected to perform at significantly lower volumes will now be hired'. (8)

Blue Cellar Combo in concert, Cheetah, 1969

139

Interior, Cheetah, 1968

The futuristic interior design made the disco an interesting backdrop for film directors. In 1969, scenes for the Jerry Cotton film *Dead Body on Broadway* were filmed in the *Cheetah*. In 1970, the opening scene featuring Heinz Erhardt in his comedy *What Is the Matter with Willi?* was filmed here.

A keen disco-goer (Uwe Lemke, who was 25 at the time) fondly recalls his many visits to the *Cheetah*: 'Up to the mid-seventies, I was there almost every weekend from about midnight with my buddies. It was a quality, trendy spot. There was some etiquette when it came to clothes: anyone wearing leather gear or t-shirts was refused entry by the bouncer. Five of us had regular seats there at a table in these fantastic round armchairs, they were like bowls. We were warmly welcomed, and scarcely had we arrived when a bottle of whiskey, cola and ice were placed on the table before us. Sometimes, Werner Lenke and his wife came by and said hello. Both were beautifully dressed: he wore a fantastic suit and her hair always looked amazing! Celebrities were also attracted to the club, and the two of them often sat drinking Champagne with people. Among the famous guests, I remember Lord Knud and Horst Nußbaum, who went by the name Jack White.

But sometimes it was so full that our seats bit the dust. Then of course there were the buses from West Germany that drove up with young tourists. The turnover must have been huge – the two waiters were permanently on the go with their trays trying to keep everyone satisfied. You could still get table service, not something you would see in any disco today. We also danced of course; the girls were still asked to dance back then, as it should be. The disc jockey stood on a circular platform to the right of the stage, which could be raised hydraulically. This meant that he could make eye contact with the various levels and encourage people to dance. The main dance floor was below in the middle. However, some people danced on the individual levels. Frank Zander performed a midnight show every Saturday in a vampire outfit. The lighting was eerie, and he performed scary writings and songs.' [19]

An extract from the list of bands that played in the *Cheetah* reads like a who's who of 1970s beat and pop music: *Scorpions* (1973); *The Searchers, Suzie Quatro* and *Bill Haley* (his last concert in Germany) (1976); *Desmond Dekker, The Tremeloes, The Drifters*, and *Dozy, Beaky, Mick & Tich* (1977).

One music manager recalled: 'When Eric Burdon or Amanda Lear performed, the place was full to the rafters. Amanda Lear claimed beforehand: I'm not coming down out of the drain! By "drain" she meant the spiral staircase that led out of the basement to the circular dance floor in the middle of the room, which also formed the stage for concerts. So a special temporary entrance with a small backstage area was quickly arranged. It was an amazing concert! At the end, everyone banged on the steel tables for an encore.'

147

149

151

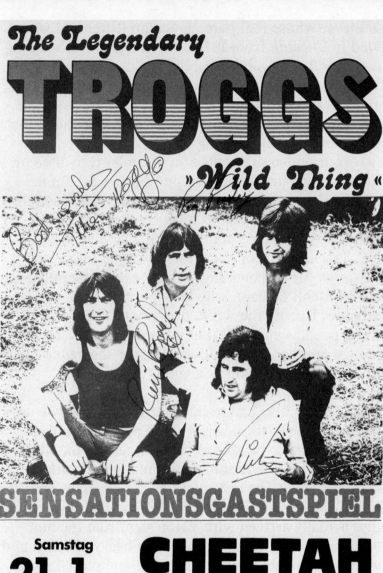

153

DJ Stevy (whose real name is Stefan Ritter and who DJed in *Cheetah* from 1976 to 1979 and is still working as a DJ today) began his career as a disc jockey in *Cheetah* – playing at events for secondary school students in 1976, when he was just 17: 'The first time, I went there with all the students from my school, that was over a thousand young people alone! After that, I gave out leaflets and touted for a regular teen disco on Sundays that started at 3.00 pm. In the end, up to 2,800 young people came every week. As it was so full, we decided to offer parties for secondary school students on Wednesdays and Thursdays as well. When I say "we", I mean the proprietor Jürgen Lenke (owner of the *Koffer-Meyer* company), Big Boss Peter Wonneberger and DJ Mehli Lentzer, who later became Managing Director. During the week, only about 1,000 or 1,500 young people came, but that was still a significant enough number. DJ Mehli was already somewhat older and was jealous of me as a young lad.' [20]

A disc jockey also had to be entertaining in those days: 'When it came to the music, I could play what I liked. But I also had to be able to create a certain mood. I organised games where someone could win a bottle of sparkling wine. The task might be, for example, who can bring me the most original object? And then five young guys actually arrived with a stop sign from the bus stop (back then the signs stood on a heavy pedestal and were not cemented into the ground) and placed it on the stage. Yikes, that was embarrassing for me. Of course, they had to take it back straight away, but they still won.' [20]

The *Berliner Morgenpost* even reported on one of these competitions: 'They sat in Kliem's (author's note: in the small hall on the neighbouring property), enjoying

Sieben runde Tanzflächen und bewegliche Sessel — wie au[s] einem alten Kinosaal die Super-Discothek „Cheetah" wurde

Manuela Groener aus Mariendorf (großes Foto) ist 17 Jahre alt — sie kommt immer an den Teenie-Tagen ins „Cheetah". Wer durch die zw[ei] Eingangsröhren aus Edelstahl (kleines Foto, links) gegangen ist, bekommt drinnen von Disc-Jockey Stevie (kleines Foto, rechts) nicht n[ur] heiße Platten serviert, es gibt auch Pizza, Buletten und Curry-Wurst für 1,50 Mark. Fotos: Bernd Pukall[a]

Von VOLKER GERTH

Berlin, 28. April

Einst war die Ha-senheide der Kudamm für Berlins Südosten —

Ballhäusern, Gartencafés und großen Kinos. Als dann ...967 der letzte Streifen über die ...einwand im alten „Primus-Pa-.ast" flimmerte, wurde aus dem ...00 Quadratmeter großen Kino-.aal ausnahmsweise kein Su-...ermarkt.

Unter Polizeischutz (wegen ...es Andrangs) drehte (damals) ...ropas modernste und größte ...

Discothek (2000 Plätze) ihre ge-waltige Musikanlage (3500 Watt) auf.

Stammgäste werden mit Handschlag begrüßt

Das „Cheetah" wurde älter, aber das Stammpublikum vom Geschäftsführer manchmal mit Handschlag und „Hallo!" begrüßt — inzwischen immer jünger.

An den „Teenie-Tagen" Mitt-woch, Donnerstag und Sonntag drängen sich ab 15 Uhr Schüle-

rinnen und Lehrlinge an der Kasse, legen die eine Mark Ein-tritt (Freitag und Samstag ko-stet's drei) oft groschenweise auf den Tisch.

Friseurlehring Michaela Schnieber (16) kommt zum Bei-spiel regelmäßig mit der U-Bahn aus Tegel. „Wegen des dürften Publikums und wegen der Teenie-Preise", sagt sie.

Und die sind ausgesprochen „taschengeldfreundlich": Cola gibt's — Selbstbedienung — für 2 Mark (sonst 2,60), Bier für 2,50 (sonst 2,80). Ein kühles Blondes

wird aber immer erst ab 18 Uhr gezapft — dann müssen näm-lich die Jüngeren (14 bis 16 Jahre) nach Hause.

Der nette Stevie spielt auch mal was Langsames

Vorher dürfen sie mit einer Sondererlaubnis des Senats auf einer der sieben runden Metall-Tanzflächen rocken. Die 16- bis 18jährigen können dann noch bis 22 Uhr auf den beweglichen Sesseln — Plexiglas, Metall und rote Kuschelkissen — sitzen bleiben.

Viele kommen mit ihrer C[li-]que, andere wegen der Mus[ik] von Disc-Jockey Stevie. D[er] spielt nämlich auch mal langsa[-]me Titel — die kann man er[st] umschlungen tanzen.

Freitag und Samstag geh[t] die Disco mit ihrem Gewirr a[us] 300 Metern Stahlträgern, an d[e-]nen — durch 12 Treppen ve[r-]bunden — 21 „Sitz-Palette[n]" frei im Raum schweben, de[...]

„Großen"

Ab 19 Uhr 30 dröhnen da[...] die acht großen und 63 klein[en] Lautsprecher, flackern über 10[...] Glühbirnen . . .

the hairdressing championship, a mature married couple, around 60 years of age. Two young people, slightly out of breath, suddenly arrived at their table: Help us please, we could win 10 marks! They told the couple that there was a bet in a nearby beat pub (the *Cheetah*) to quickly find a couple who could do an excellent waltz. But the waltz wasn't something the younger generation could do. The married couple didn't need to be asked twice. The charming hairdressing competition was exchanged for the buzzing disco in the neighbouring building. When the waltz was played by the disc jockey, the old-timers performed their dance for the young audience with style.

In addition to winning their bet, the young people had also won the favour of their "victims": not only with the glass of sparkling wine they bought the older dancers but more from the sheer fun factor of this bet. "It's so nice when the young people include us older ones now and then in their fun in such a lovely way", the couple commented.'

But not everything that happened was fun: 'When the disco era began with *Saturday Night Fever*, I was in the right place at the right time with my teen parties. Straight away we got ourselves a big disco ball and hung it 12 metres above the floor. One Sunday, the attachment for the ball loosened and this heavy thing plummeted onto the jam-packed dance floor! Thankfully, nothing happened. It's frightening to think that it could have killed someone. Most of the people there didn't even notice.' (20)

The DJ himself faced several sticky situations: 'To get into my round disco cockpit, I had to climb up a vertical "henhouse ladder". At the base of the cockpit there was a motor that operated a cable to raise and lower the cockpit. One time, in 1979, I raised it up, but something wasn't quite right. When I wanted to carefully lower the cockpit again by pressing a button, the steel cable snapped and the cockpit came crashing down. Luckily, however, there was a suspension system and I was OK. I thought first that I had done something wrong. Most of the records had fallen off and the turntable was tilted but it was still working. To avoid any commotion, I put on a new record straight away and most of the people there didn't notice anything. Mr Wonneberger naturally got a huge fright and from that day on, the cockpit was never moved again.

Another time, I was almost a goner. The big parabolic mirrors, which were about 3 metres in diameter, were fitted with bulbs. One time, I simply screwed in stronger 100-watt bulbs that lit up to the rhythm of the music. It looked wild. But as I was standing there on a high ladder, the manager came over and shouted: Leave that and come straight down here! I found out then that the connections for the bulbs had not been fused; I was lucky!' (20)

An irritated neighbour complained: 'At the weekend, it was bursting at the seams. Hundreds of young people were waiting on the street at the entrance. Then nothing could move out the front. There were just parked cars everywhere, we couldn't get in or out. We got the registration numbers of the cars that needed to be moved and had the owners paged.' (21)

Even the tabloid newspaper *Bild* deemed the swarming crowds worth a report: 'On the "Teenie days" – Wednesdays, Thursdays and Sundays – secondary school students and apprentices throng the ticket desk from 3.00 pm in the afternoon, paying their 1 mark entrance fee (3 marks on a Friday or Saturday), often in groschens.' (Back then, 1 groschen was a 10-pfennig coin.) Even the drink prices were extremely 'pocket money-friendly: a self-service cola costs 2 marks. A cold beer is only on tap from 6.00 pm – the younger ones (14- to 16-year-olds) have to head home then. (…) The 16- to 18-year-olds can stay around until 10.00 pm to enjoy the movable armchairs, which are made from plexiglass and metal and decorated with cosy red cushions. Many come with their pals, others come to hear the music played by Stevy, the disc jockey. He also plays slow tracks from time to time, allowing couples to dance in a close embrace. On Fridays and Saturdays, the disco belongs to the adults. They navigate its maze of 300-metre steel beams on which 21 seated platforms, connected by twelve steps, float freely in space. From 7.30 pm, the eight large and 63 small loudspeakers blast out the music, synchronised with 1,000 flickering bulbs.' (*Bild*, 28 April 1978)

159

Entrance, Cheetah, 1978

162

163

With these numbers of people, it was inevitable that the interior would suffer: a former patron was later 'disappointed by the general state (author's note: of the premises): there were burn holes in the carpet; the plexiglass was grubby and shabby, noticeably neglected. Such a pity.' The management and the clientele also changed, but not for the better: 'The *Cheetah* was a really top place in the beginning. Back then, it was run by El Raab, an agricultural machinery engineer who came from Egypt. He was a very charming, charismatic, modest – he drove a Volkswagen Beetle – and quiet person. The DJ at the time was called Mehli, I don't know what his real name was. El Raab subsequently went back to his home country. Under his successor, who drove up straight away in a Mercedes 450 E, standards went rapidly downhill: the former dress code no longer existed – people now also came in wearing scruffy-looking gear – and slowly but surely other standards of behaviour, including my own, also deteriorated.' (22)

In 1979, the number of club-goers dropped significantly, from a monthly figure of 18,000 to only about half of that, and management let a number of employees go. This also included DJ Stevy, who subsequently managed to win compensation by bringing a case to an employment tribunal.

In 1980, the Senate finally ceased to grant a special permit for the afternoon disco for under-16s. This deprived the *Cheetah* of a major source of income. Furnishings in the temple of dance were also somewhat outdated. Lastly, the complaints of residents did not abate: 'For us immediate neighbours, the weekend discos caused a great deal of annoyance. The doors were frequently left open and there wasn't enough soundproofing. It was mega loud. The tenants in the first courtyard, where at that time there wasn't even a dividing wall with the neighbouring property, suffered particularly badly. We complained, and the building inspectorate took measurements in our apartments. The inspectorate then imposed certain conditions, but they were not complied with.' (21)

All of these adverse circumstances led to the closure of the club in July 1983. The following notice advertising its sale appeared in the daily Berlin press: 'Large Berlin discotheque, famous throughout the country and still popular. Bars and dance floors on three levels, with an area of approx. 650 square metres available for guests. Skylift disco, large stage for live events, etc. Asking price 450,000, negotiable (official turnover tax regulations apply), partial financing or buy to lease possible, viewing by appointment.'

Sector Tanzpalast Kreuzberg
1984—1988

No buyer or new leaseholder was found for the *Cheetah* disco, only other operators were brought in. The ballroom was renovated by *Jürgen Lenke & Lehmann Gaststättenbetriebs GmbH* although this involved little or no alterations to the building; only the soundproofing was improved. With a new, up-market name (*Sector – Tanzpalast Kreuzberg*), the intention was probably to conceal the location's proximity to Neukölln, a somewhat disreputable area. Kreuzberg, on the other hand, had by now become *the* hip district in West Berlin. This new beginning looked promising. Well-known 1980s bands performed, among them *Duran Duran, Ina Deter, Gruppo Sportivo*, and *Einstürzende Neubauten*.

'A band played almost every day – it was sensational. After about two months, the excitement had died down and DM 200,000 had to be found. Since then, it's just been pure, unadulterated disco. Clomp, clomp – from left to right and back again. Hard disco is the sound on offer here – but never hit parade. (...) Both disc jockeys bought new records for the kids (with an average age of 20) each week at a cost of 500 to 600 marks. But that was still cheaper than having a band, as the Managing Director Peter Wonneberger found.' (23)

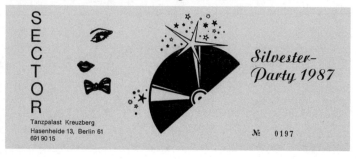

Discothek **SECTOR** Discothek

1000 Berlin 61 · Hasenheide 13

Silvester-Party '86

N⁰ 0591   Einlaß: 19.oo Uhr
Eintritt: 10,— DM

People will always argue over taste in music. DJ Double T
(whose real name is Thorsten Prange and who DJed in
Sector in 1987/88), however, liked the selection that was
played in the *Sector*: 'The great thing about that place
was that it had a real mix of people, but hardly any
tourists, unlike the discos on the Kudamm. The music
was equally mixed. Different types of music were played
in blocks: from rockabilly to disco and new wave, from
hard rock to punk. I thought it was awesome!' (24)

Angela Harting, a *Sector* patron who was 17 at the time
was similarly enthusiastic: 'On Sunday afternoons, I
used to travel in from Rudow to go dancing in the *Sector*
on Hermannplatz. The dance floors were on several
levels and there were gaming and pinball machines in
the corners. I loved it when the fog wafted through the
various levels and I could hear my music. It was cheap:
you could get everything for one mark. I could spend
a few hours here before I had to make the long journey
home. But dancing? That's probably a bit of an exag-
geration! With a few discreet, jerky movements, we
made our way into the middle of the dance floor and
back again. Everyone was cool and dressed in black.
I always wore very tight, long, black skirts so I could
take only very small steps. I also wore fingerless gloves.
I had white makeup on my face, my eyes were accen-
tuated in black, my hair was back-combed with a neon

green streak. Obviously, I only got dressed up like this once I had left the house.' (25)

Anyone who was under 18 had to show their ID at the entrance: 'These were very carefully scrutinised. Then they (author's note: the under-18s) had to be collected by midnight at the latest, otherwise their names would be called out over the PA system. That was embarrassing of course, and nobody wanted that.' (24)

The Berlin-based producer Peter Powalla organised talent competitions in the *Sector*. *C. C. Catch* appeared on one of these shows and later became very famous. Even *Prince* is said to have turned up in the *Sector* after his concert in 1987. Films were also made here, including a scene from the 1988 film *Judgment in Berlin*, in which Ted Herold appeared.

Joe an der Hasenheide
1989—1993

In retrospect, the *Sector* years were like an interlude, like a last chance to save what could no longer be saved. A new era began for the disco in 1989. The well-known restaurateur, Detlef 'Joe' Gerhardt, who was already running several successful large restaurants in West Berlin, took over the lease. He had a new idea for the run-down temple of dance on Hasenheide. He planned a 'master disco' for an over-40s, more affluent clientele.

Free ticket, Joe, 1990

Following extensive renovations that cost around 6 million deutschmarks, *Joe an der Hasenheide* opened in 1989. It was said that the laser system was the biggest in Europe at that time and that the sound system alone, which had been flown in from the US, cost 3 million deutschmarks.

The blurb wasn't short on superlatives either: 'Capacity – 2,500 guests, sound – 11,000 watts, lighting – 15 Jupiter lights and more, seven bars on three levels, brilliant, exclusive science fiction ambience, international show programmes and top acts'.

The pub and cultural guide *Berlin zwischen Sekt und Selters* quipped in 1990: 'Super Joe: almost everything here is super. Through the mirror-clad tunnels into the valley of dance friends. You enter a strange space-ship and need to get your bearings. At the front on the right, there is a super dance music show. Lead dancers show you how it's done. Climb the stairs. Everywhere there are red seating areas that are a really super match for the red bow ties worn by the staff. The department store, bank and insurance employees clap ecstatically with freshly manicured hands. Everyone thinks it is suuuuuper.' (26)

At weekends, admission cost between 15 and 20 deutsch-marks, unusually high for the Kreuzberg and Neukölln areas. On Sundays, concerts that catered specially for the over-40s were hosted: in addition to singers as diverse as *Roland Kaiser* and *Phil Collins*, German rock band *The Lords* also celebrated their 30th anniversary at the club.

Thorsten Prange, who had worked as a DJ in the prede-cessor club, compared the atmosphere in both venues: 'At *Joe's* it was much classier. The crowd was somewhat older and not as mixed as during the *Sector* days: in the past, Turkish colleagues had also still worked there, on the door, and even punks weren't turned away.

173

That all changed. The *Sector* was more run-down, now it had become a fancy-schmancy kind of place. It was also more expensive, and somehow that didn't suit the locality: this joint should have been on the Kudamm, it might have survived for longer there.' (24)

However, Marcos López, one of the DJs at *Joe's*, didn't find such a major difference between *Joe's* and its predecessor, the *Sector*. In an interview with *dt64* – the youth station that had survived its East German past – in 1991, he described his impressions: 'The music is as colourful as the crowd is diverse, and one is a reason for the other. I can put together a crazy mix of tracks there, precisely because the crowd is so crazy. I couldn't just play house or just play techno, people would chuck the lemons from their Bacardi and cokes at me! The crowd here is not a typical party crowd that rocks up with whistles, glow sticks and sunglasses to party at the weekend every fortnight. It is a relatively normal clientele that enjoys well-presented music without being too fixated with the charts. I can sell them a lot of off-beat music. Granted, the location is a bit too sterile and clean but at least it's not as grotty and druggy as many other places. *Joe's* is definitely a cool place, some good people work there, we really rock out, but hardly anyone would realise that from the hip people there. It's all about the music and the partying, that's all that matters, and that's what the people do here.'

Some of the special events, however, were not to everyone's taste or they only appealed to a very specific audience. In October 1992, for example, the *Miss Berlin* competition had 23 contestants, and in April 1993, the *Mister Berlin* competition had 16 contestants. Under the headline 'Who is the most beautiful man in the country?', the *tageszeitung*, the Berlin daily newspaper,

175

commented: 'What motivates him and 15 other men, among them car mechanics, students, toolmakers and a 38-year-old underground train driver, to spend hundreds of marks on a suit and tie and an expensive designer body and to show up on this Easter Sunday in the laser beam at the *Joe Hasenheide* discotheque? For some, it is the hope of a fun evening in front of friends and family, for others it is the result of a lost bet. (...) The contest to find the most beautiful man in Berlin proceeds according to a strictly choreographed ceremony. The dramatic sounds of trumpets and drums herald the appearance of all 16 contestants. Although they were given free rein with their choice of clothing in the first round of the competition, sports jackets, shoes with a perforated pattern, ties and pleated trousers dominate. Even the jackets in a selection of colours ranging from bright orange to a delicate mint green do nothing to change the oddly uniform appearance of numbers 1 to 16. (...) Mainly young girls with dyed or back-combed hair wait interminably, a few metres in front of the stage, not letting their favourite contestants out of their sight.' (Barbara Bollwahn, in the *tageszeitung*, 13 April 1993)

As an experienced restaurateur, Joe noticed very quickly that his disco concept did not have a chance of surviving very long at this location, and in 1993 he relaunched the entertainment venue.

From Pleasure Dome to collapse
1993—1996

While Joe Gerhardt's name continued to be on the lease, two music managers – Reinhard Konzack and Wolfgang Merten – took over the management of the club, which was renamed the *Pleasure Dome*. It was aimed once again at a younger clientele and the admission price was reduced to 10 euro.

In August 1993, *Der Tagesspiegel* wrote: 'The new operators limited the renovation of the grandfathered building mainly to the entrance: it gleams in shining silver. Inside, it is mainly the lighting system that has been re-vamped. Bright lights that flashed in a smooth rhythm may have been good enough for the *Cheetah*, today, process-controlled lighting technology and video projections reign supreme. Two laser beams project their focused light onto the mirrored struts, from which it bounces straight through the room.' (*Der Tagesspiegel*, 6 August 1993)

In parallel with the disco nights, events reminiscent of Joe Gerhardt's time also took place. In January 1994, for example, a live recording was made of the TV game show *Alles dran nebenan*, screened by the regional TV broadcaster *IA Brandenburg*. The event was derided by the *tageszeitung*: 'Ulrich Schamoni's local TV is aiming for frivolity: because everyone in the world of IA is keen to finally catch sight of the buxom neighbour naked at the window, the IA scouts have travelled to country discos and have propositioned various neighbours. So this is how Katrin ended up on the programme, with a plunging neckline and a badge with her name on it attached above her bosom, sitting with five other women beside Sven Blümel. The host doles out lollipops as points. In one game, Katrin is allowed to "lick clean" a pane of glass or take an IA sticker out of a terrarium with cockroaches in it. Then the contestants

climb into the ever-threatening pool in their swimsuits.
Down on your knees now, like when you were a child and
you played puppies, orders Blümel. And booming from
the loudspeakers: This is the saucy girl from the neighbourhood. She is so hot that she even gives the neighbour
a hard time. With a shaky camera, dreadful sound and
without any narrative, IA wants to suggest to us that we
are in dad's basement party room.' (*tageszeitung*,
20 January 1994)

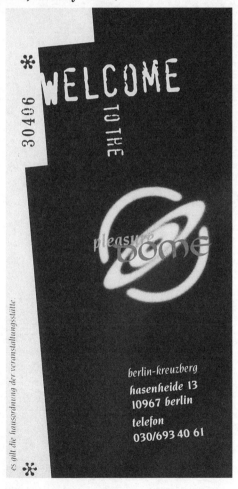

Ticket, *Pleasure Dome*, 1995

Even the Sunday singles parties with 'messengers of love' or fashion club parties did not exude a big city aura: 'The club has something very timeless, very ordinary. No trends are set here. Instead, the DJs rely on a proven mix of chart music and older disco sounds. The clientele is very mixed and not really defined in terms of a particular scene. You could almost say that it is a type of suburban disco, allowing anyone who wants to come in'. (*Der Tagesspiegel,* 6 July 1996)

The dancing and shows finally came to an end in 1996. Joe Gerhardt had to declare bankruptcy, complaining that: 'we never recouped the 6 million'. The new competitors in the former East Berlin – *Bunker, E-Werk,* and *Tresor* – were not the only reason why things went downhill at Hasenheide. On the one hand, the club was somewhat too fancy in terms of furnishings. On the other hand, it was somewhat too 'ordinary' when it came to the clientele, which was also due to its location on the border of Neukölln, at that time still a 'chavvy' district. It was therefore always disparagingly dismissed by the young Berlin hipsters. Moreover, compared to some small German towns, large-capacity discos rarely did well in Berlin, unless they were in largely unrenovated industrial buildings. The location on Hasenheide, however, was a fancy, high-tech temple. At the same time, after the fall of the Berlin Wall, many dance fans had moved on to the newly established clubs in the former East Berlin: Kreuzberg was (temporarily) 'out', Mitte, Prenzlauer Berg, and Friedrichshain, on the other hand, were 'hip'.

More and more new ideas
1996—2019

In 1996, the Munich-based company *Hypo-Real Haus- und Grundbesitz GmbH & Co. Immobilien-Vermietungs KG,* purchased Hasenheide 13, but sold it again two years later. The new owner was the recently established *Grundstücksgemeinschaft Hasenheide 13 GbR,* which had three partners. In 1998, the buyers undertook a challenging project. Uli Mente, one of those involved in the project outlines the plans: 'It was to be the biggest gay sauna in Europe. We kept the circular platforms in the hall and built cabins on top of them that were kitted out with mattresses. The basement was converted into a sauna and tiled in black as a darkroom.' (27)

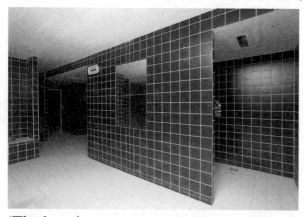

'The location was supposed to be called *Aquarius Sauna.* A flight of stairs led from the sauna in the basement to the bar on the ground floor. A large jacuzzi had been installed on the former stage and this could be accessed via a spiral staircase from the basement. Beside it was a Champagne bar. While there were detailed building plans, there wasn't enough money to actually make them a reality. The construction work was always financed on a piecemeal basis using loans.' (28)

A gay bar, *Ficken 3000*, opened at Urbanstraße 70 around the same time: 'All the furnishings there came from the *Pleasure Dome*. This meant that the bar could open after just three months of construction work. That place did really well.' (28) The income earned in the bar went into the development of the sauna club at Hasenheide. *Aquarius Betriebs GmbH* was also set up. From 1998, its leaseholders ran the *Aquarius* café in the former entrance area of the disco where the metal tunnels were located.

Erkan Gezer, one of the two bar operators, remembers: 'All the furnishings in the bar also came from the former disco, the *Pleasure Dome*. They were removed from there and installed here. I upholstered the old orange seats in a jungle-style fabric. The owners wanted me to call the café *Aquarius*, it was to be the same name as the subsequent sauna club. But I didn't like the name, and in 2000 I finally renamed it *Café Cheetah* but one year later, I gave it up.' (28)

The ambitious sauna club project failed because of differences between the partners. One of the shareholders was deceitful and had in fact gone broke before the project even began. 2 million deutschmarks were allegedly 'lost' before the bank refused to extend additional credit, even though only the fire protection and emergency power supply system had to be completed.

Despite the unfinished state of construction of the former disco – or precisely because of it – other film people used the location as an interesting set. A music video for *Sarah Connor* was filmed here, and a documentary released in 2019 about the Schlager singer *Ricky Shayne*, who had performed at the launch of *Cheetah*. The latter included scenes that show the interior of the club in the background, still covered in construction dust, around 2000.

In 2004, forced administration was finally imposed and two years later the site, including the almost-complete sauna club, came under the hammer. *Taekker Achte Grundbesitz GmbH* purchased the property at auction for 1.4 million euro.

Meanwhile, the *Tunnel* bar had existed as the successor to *Café Cheetah* since 2002. The name of course referred to the long, fully mirrored tunnel entrance to the former disco. Unfortunately, the leaseholder, Mustafa 'Musti' Tasdemir, had trustingly paid his rent in advance without signing a contract and lost his 'rent-free' entitlement during the change of ownership. As *Taekker* deemed the entrance necessary for any new potential tenants of the hall, Tasdemir was given notice as a precautionary measure in 2007.

Exterior, *Tunnel*, around 2005

A number of daring entrepreneurs with no less daring project ideas did actually come forward. One of them wanted to open a pool hall, with a pool table located on each of the old platforms. The question, however, was how to make it profitable: nobody could play so much pool that it would cover the heating costs, which would be considerable for this huge premises. Another interested party, who wanted to open another disco here, also abandoned his project. Finally, a dubious investor rented the entire establishment and purported to complete the sauna club. However, after rent arrears accumulated, he disappeared without a trace.

In 2010, *Taekker* lost patience. Detlef Steffen, the caretaker at the time, experienced the consequences: 'Because no new tenant could be found, a decision was made to demolish the steel frames and platforms in the old disco. It was hoped that it would be easier to rent out an empty space and a company was found that would remove these structures free of charge. This company benefited from the proceeds made by selling the steel scrap. But even after that, a tenant couldn't be found. Even though lots of people were interested, most of them were just interested in a part of the huge space.' (29)

189

During the demolition, the *KitKatClub* illegally used the lower level where the large counter still stood (some of the platforms had already been removed) for four weeks over the Easter period. Then the demolition sacrilege was complete: in August 2010, the ballroom was emptied and historically significant interior furnishings were permanently removed. The two tunnel openings facing the street were also demolished.

While the former bar in the front building found a tenant in 2013 in the form of the *Berlino* pizzeria, *Taekker* submitted an application in the same year to demolish the Saalgebäude and build a new block of apartments. However, the owner of the neighbouring site at Hasenheide 12 objected to the demolition as he feared negative consequences for the fabric of the building on his property. The building inspectorate did not approve the plans for the new building, as it exceeded the size of the area for which development was permitted. *Taekker* submitted an objection to the official decision but withdrew it in 2015.

In 2016, the ballroom was temporarily rented to *Urban Industrial* for two years. The two owners, Tigran Tatintsian and Jakob Wagner, used the premises as a showroom for the industrial furniture they were selling ('industrial lamps, furniture & rare objects'). The two resourceful young entrepreneurs were delighted with their new home: 'Previously, we were in two railway arches on Holzmarktstraße but the rent was too high for us there. A customer told us about a ballroom on Hasenheide that was 800 square metres. A friend of mine, who lives at Hasenheide 12, said that he didn't know of any such ballroom there. It's true that you can't see it from the road! But we finally got in touch with *Taekker* when the situation got very urgent for us. Everything went very quickly after that: on Thursday, 5 August 2016, we signed the contract and the next day we had the keys. We rented the hall as a storeroom and showroom in order to have a wider range of options for its use. As the demolition was planned, we only got a rental agreement for two years. The rent was 3,000 euro per month.' (30)

At this point, the entire interior was still clad with a blue painted wire plaster wall and in the middle of the ball-room there was still a big hole with a spiral staircase leading to the basement. The two new tenants then 'set to work with two punks. We tore out all the ugly wire plaster walls to expose the brick walls. Using a lifting platform that just about fit through the back door, we started at the top with an electric circular saw and stripped the walls. It was a really hazardous job. We only kept the stage. It was only then that we moved in. We had 15 to 20 truckloads, going back and forth. They were extremely stressful weeks as we were still working in the old shop at the same time.' (30)

Interior, Hasenheide 13, 2016

Photos of how *Urban Industrial* used the space show how well the company was suited to the location and how successfully the vintage items available for sale were arranged in the hall. A feast for the eyes! Nevertheless, it was clear to everyone involved that it was only a temporary use because the rental agreement expired in 2018. A last chance to save the ballroom in its existing form and, where possible, to facilitate a longer-term rental agreement, was seen in the attempt to make the ballroom a listed building. Although fragments of the interesting changes undergone by the ballroom are visible to this day – the existence of the stage and the rest of the wall painting dating back to 1900, the hatches for the cinema projectors, and the remains of the steel struts from the disco era – this was not reason enough for the Antiquities and Monuments Office.

As the property had not changed hands in over ten years (which made selling it a particularly tax-efficient option) and as the demolition permit and approval for a new building were still valid (making the property even more valuable) *Taekker* put Hasenheide 13 up for sale. It was a stroke of luck that the Herford-based entrepreneur and art collector Heiner Wemhöner heard about the sale and immediately began to negotiate. He had been looking for a Berlin property that had enough space for him to exhibit the works in his collection. Consequently, it was not his intention to tear down the old ballroom, nor was he interested in constructing an extensive new building. Nevertheless, a considerable sum was required for payment. The purchase agreement was registered on 5 September 2018 and a promising, sustainable future began for the 120-year-old ballroom.

193

Appendix

Literature/Sources

1 Paetel, Paul, 'In der Hasenheide zu Großvaters Zeiten', *Die Luisenstadt: Ein Heimatbuch*, Berlin, 1927.
2 *Die Gartenlaube*, Berlin, 1866.
3 Reinmar, Walter, *Berliner Kinder: Bunte Bilder aus der Reichshauptstadt*, Berlin, 1888.
4 Schaeffer, Paul, *Vor dem Halleschen Tore*, Berlin, 1913.
6 Landesarchiv Berlin (Bauakten Hasenheide 14/15, Akten der Theaterpolizei, Strafverfahren des Generalstaatsanwalts).
7 Lengemann, Simon, *Nacht-Depesche*, Berlin, ca. 1970.
8 Bauaktenarchiv des Bezirksamts Friedrichshain Kreuzberg (Bauakten Hasenheide 13).
9 Piscator, Erwin, *Die Briefe: 1960–1966* (vol. 3.3), Berlin, 2011.
10 Piscator, Erwin, *Das Proletarische Theater*, Berlin, 1929.
11 Brandenburgisches Landeshauptarchiv (Akten der Abt. III des Polizei-Präsidiums zu Berlin).
12 E. Lindemann, 1989, as cited in Kolland, Dorothea (ed.); Kunstamt Neukölln, *Rixdorfer Musen, Neinsager und Caprifischer: Musik und Theatergeschichte aus Rixdorf und Neukölln*, Berlin, 1990.
13 Aitken, Robbie, *Berlins Schwarzer Kommunist*, Berlin, 2019 (online only).
14 Lengemann, Simon, '"Erst das Essen, dann die Miete!": Protest und Selbsthilfe in Berliner Arbeitervierteln während der Großen Depression 1931 bis 1933', *Jahrbuch für Forschungen zur Geschichte der Arbeiterbewegung*, no. 3 (2015).
16 Hänsel, Sylvaine; Schmitt, Angelika (eds.), *Kinoarchitektur in Berlin 1895–1995*, Berlin, 1995.
18 *Südost-Express*, Berlin, January 1986.
23 *Blickpunkt*, Berlin, January 1984.
26 *Berlin zwischen Sekt und Selters*, Cadolzburg, 1992.

Contemporary witnesses/
Interview partners

17 Friedrich Uebel
19 Uwe Lemke
20 Stefan Ritter (DJ Stevy)
21 Ole Schnack
22 R. T. on abriss-berlin.de
24 Thorsten Prange (DJ Double T)
25 Angela Harting
27 Uli Mente
28 Erkan Gezer
29 Detlef Steffen
30 Jakob Wagner

Explanatory notes

5 The Ruthe was comparable to the English rod and was subdivided in different ways. It was of different lengths, depending on the location.
15 ADGB = Allgemeiner Deutscher Gewerkschaftsbund (General German Trade Union Federation); RGO = Revolutionäre Gewerkschafts Opposition (Revolutionary Union Opposition).

Further sources

- *Berliner Tageblatt*, 2 May 1929.
- *Berliner Stadtadressbuch*, Berlin, 1861–1943.
- *Berlinische Nachrichten von Staats und gelehrten Sachen*, Berlin, 1812.
- Bernstein, Eduard, *Die Berliner Arbeiterbewegung* (3 vols.). Berlin, 1907, 1910.
- *Bild*, 28 April 1978.
- von Chézy, Helmina, *Erinnerungen aus meinem Leben*, Berlin, 1917.
- *Die Rote Fahne*, various volumes from 1920 onwards.
- Dominik, Emil, *Quer durch und ringsum Berlin*, Berlin, 1883.
- Heinrich-Jost, Ingrid, *Auf ins Metropol: Specialitäten und Unterhaltungstheater im ausgehenden 19. Jahrhundert*, Berlin, 1987.
- Jansen, Wolfgang, *Das Varieté: Die glanzvolle Geschichte einer unterhaltenden Kunst*, Berlin, 1990.
- Jansen, Wolfgang; Lorenzen, Rudolf, *Possen, Piefke und Posaunen: Sommertheater und Gartenkonzerte in Berlin*, Berlin, 1987.
- Lange, Annemarie, *Berlin zur Zeit Bebels und Bismarcks*, Berlin, 1984.
- Lange, Annemarie, *Berlin in der Weimarer Republik*, Berlin, 1987.
- *Neuköllner Tageblatt*, various volumes from 1912 onwards.
- Piscator, Erwin, *Die Briefe: 1909–1936* (vol. 1), Berlin, 2005.
- *Rixdorfer Zeitung*, various volumes from 1900 onwards.
- Schrader, Tillmann; Uebel, Lothar; Heimatmuseum Neukölln (eds.), *Eine große Familie: Artisten und ihre Vereine in Neukölln*, Berlin, 1986.
- Schwerk, Ekkehard, *Berlin wie es keiner kennt*, Berlin, 1975.
- *Der Tagesspiegel*, various volumes from 1960 onwards.
- *tageszeitung*, various volumes from 1990 onwards.
- Tomisch, Jürgen; Landesdenkmalamt Berlin, *Gutachten zum Denkmalwert*, Berlin, 1996 (unpublished)

- Uebel, Lothar, *Viel Vergnügen: Die Geschichte der Vergnügungsstätten am Kreuzberg und an der Hasenheide*, Berlin, 1985.
- Uebel, Lothar, *Die Neue Welt an der Hasenheide: Über hundert Jahre Vergnügen und Politik*, Berlin, 1994.
- Uebel, Lothar, *Vom Hofjäger zur Villa Hasenheide*, Berlin, 1996.
- *Vorwärts*, various volumes from 1899 onwards.
- *Vossische Zeitung*, 2 May 1929.

- Archiv der Akademie der Künste
- Archiv der sozialen Demokratie der Friedrich-Ebert Stiftung
- Bibliothek des Vereins für die Geschichte Berlins
- Bundesarchiv
- Deutsche Kinemathek
- Deutsches Historisches Museum
- Domäne Dahlem
- Grundbuchaktenarchiv im Amtsgericht Tempelhof-Kreuzberg
- Friedrichshain-Kreuzberg Museum
- Museum Neukölln
- Sammlung Jansen
- Sammlung Klünner
- Sammlung Uebel
- Staatsbibliothek zu Berlin
- Stadtbibliothek Neukölln
- Stiftung Stadtmuseum Berlin
- Untere Denkmalschutzbehörde Friedrichshain Kreuzberg
- Verein für die Geschichte Berlins e. V.
- Zentrum für Berlin-Studien

List of images

akg – Archiv für Kunst und Geschichte, Berlin

p. 86

A Piscator Archive (EPS, Sign. 38991)

p. 62

Archiv der Jugendkulturen

p. 146

Archiv der Sozialen Demokratie / Friedrich-Ebert-Stiftung, Berlin

p. 124

p. 125

Geheimes Staatsarchiv Preußischer Kulturbesitz, Berlin

pp. 16–17

Joachim Barfknecht © picture alliance RM

pp. 136–137 and cover

Bauaktenarchiv des Bezirksamts Friedrichshain-Kreuzberg, Berlin

pp. 30–31

p. 39

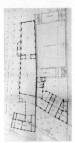

p. 40

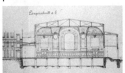

p. 41

p. 41

p. 115

Bundesarchiv, Berlin

p. 71

pp. 92–93

Deutsche Kinemathek, Berlin

p. 112

Bildarchiv Preußischer Kulturbesitz, Berlin

pp. 24–25 and back cover

p. 47 (SPD meeting, 1913)

Erkan Gezer

p. 188

Ingo Heine

p. 192

p. 192

pp. 194–195

Kasper Jensen

p. 186

p. 191

p. 191

Landesarchiv Berlin

pp. 18–19

p. 56

p. 57

p. 58

p. 59

p. 68

p. 70

p. 80

p. 100

p. 100

p. 100

p. 114

pp. 116–117

pp. 118–119

p. 120

p. 122

pp. 140–141

pp. 142–143

pp. 144–145

p. 165

Uli Mente

p. 189

Museum Neukölln, Berlin

p. 34

Stadtbibliothek Neukölln, Berlin

p. 36

p. 36

p. 85

p. 86

p. 102

p. 104

Thorsten Prange (DJ Double T)

p. 168

p. 169

p. 172

Bernd Pukallus

p. 155

Stefan Ritter (DJ Stevy)

p. 129 (Entrance, *Cheetah*,
around 1970)

pp. 130–131

p. 133

p. 133

p. 134

p. 135

p. 148

p. 149

p. 149

p. 151

p. 152

p. 152

p. 153

p. 156

p. 159

pp. 160–161

p. 162

p. 163

Sammlung H. W., Herford

pp. 44–45

p. 51

p. 50

p. 105

Sammlung Klünner

p. 33

p. 35

p. 48

p. 105

Sammlung Uebel, Berlin

p. 26

p. 42

p. 43

p. 43

p. 120

p. 179

Sammlung Wannemacher

p. 64

Dieter Schaal (musician)

p. 138

p. 139

© Scherl / Süddeutsche Zeitung Photo

pp. 106–107

p. 108

p. 109

Rolf Schulten

p. 174

pp. 180–181

pp. 182–183

Staatsbibliothek zu Berlin

p. 15

p. 63

Stadtmuseum Berlin

pp. 82–83

p. 90

p. 90

p. 95

p. 95

p. 96

p. 96

Süddeutsche Zeitung Foto, Munich

pp. 52–53

The Heartfield Community of Heirs /
VG Bild-Kunst, Bonn 2020

p. 61 (Scene from Lajos Barta's *Russia's Day*, set design by John Heartfield)

Lothar Uebel

p. 11

© Ullstein Bild – Lehnartz

p. 51

p. 126

p. 127

www.flickr.com, Historische
Luftaufnahmen Hermannplatz
1928, Berlin

p. 80

www.rockinberlin.de

p. 150

If, despite our efforts to identify all image rights, the image rights of individuals have been infringed or the rights holders have not been correctly identified, we apologise for this.

The author and editors would like to thank:

Natalie Bayer
Heidi Börner
Julia Dilger
Stephan Dörschel
Martin Düspohl
Herrn Engel
Erkan Gezer
Dr Udo Gößwald
Frank Grothe
Gülay Gün
Theresa Hartherz
Angela Harting
Erika Hausotter
Ingo Heine
Klaus Janetzki
Dr Wolfgang Jansen
Doris Kleilein
Christa Klünner
Alfred Knoll
Martina Landmann
Uwe Lemke †
Detlef Luchterhand
Gabriele Lutterbeck
Wolfgang Mende
Uli Mente
Regina Müller
Thorsten Prange (DJ Double T)
Frank Redieß
Kristin Rieber
Stefan Ritter (DJ Stevy)
Anna-Maria Roch
Lisa Roth
Dieter Schaal
Prof. Dr Uwe Schaper
Ole Schnack
Daniel Schneider
Karl-Heinz Schubert
Rolf Schulten
Detlef Steffen
Pit Stenkhoff
Ute Strauß
Tom Tietz
Ulrike Treziak
Hans de Vos
Jakob Wagner
Dr Klaus Wannemacher
Robert Wein
Katja Wollenberg

The author would like to thank in particular his wife, Sigrid Ludwig, for her patience and sympathetic reading of the manuscript.

211

Imprint

© 2024 by jovis Verlag
An imprint of Walter de Gruyter GmbH,
Berlin/Boston. Texts by kind permission
of the authors. Pictures by kind permission of the photographers/holders of
the picture rights.

Editor:
Philipp Bollmann,
Sammlung Wemhöner

Historical research,
text and photo editing:
Lothar Uebel

Translation:
Ann Marie Bohan

Proofreading:
Cecilia Tricker

Design:
Neue Gestaltung, Berlin
www.neuegestaltung.de

Typefaces:
High Life, Fabian Harb
Monument Grotesk, Dinamo Typefaces

Paper:
Munken Print White 15

Printing and binding:
DZA Druckerei zu Altenburg

Bibliographic information published
by the Deutsche Nationalbibliothek:
The Deutsche Nationalbibliothek
lists this publication in the Deutsche
Nationalbibliografie; detailed
bibliographic data are available on
the internet at http://dnb.d-nb.de

jovis Verlag
Genthiner Straße 13
10785 Berlin

www.jovis.de

jovis books are available worldwide in
select bookstores. Please contact your
nearest bookseller or visit www.jovis.de
for information concerning your local
distribution.

ISBN 978-3-98612-097-9